More Praise for *Why Motivating People Doesn't Work...And What Does*

"I encourage leaders to read this book—but with a warning. They may get more than they expect. I learned as much about my own motivation as I did about the motivation of those I lead."
—**M. Paula Daoust, PhD, Director, Blue Cross and Blue Shield of Kansas**

"If you believe, as I do, that people are learners who long to grow, enjoy their work, be productive, make positive contributions, and build lasting relationships, then you must read this book. Susan presents tools you can use to create a company sure to unleash everyone's full potential."
—**Dick Lyles, CEO, Origin Entertainment**

"We all want help to motivate the people we lead, to help them develop and grow in a productive working environment. Susan Fowler's technique shows you the right approach, leading to both the best performance and employee commitment."
—**Agnes Jeanbart, Facilities Manager, Gulf, Unilever**

"If you read only one book this year, read this one!"
—**Robert L. Lorber, PhD, President, The Lorber Kamai Consulting Group**

"Susan reveals that the recipe for motivation does not consist of carrots and sticks. Her formula has helped me lead my patients, my employees, and myself in the joyful pursuit of healthier outcomes. I would prescribe her book to everyone!"
—**Laura Lee Copeland, MD, MBA, FACEP, emergency physician and Director of Medical Informatics, Humber River Hospital, Toronto, Canada**

"One of the greatest opportunities for leaders is to help their people create meaning. Susan's book shows us how."
—**Mine Sadiç, EEMEA Training Development Manager, Roche, Istanbul, Turkey**

"Ever wonder what makes your consumers, clients, business partners, and employees keep coming back? Susan opens your eyes to why they do and how you can make the choice to return easy."
—**Tom Porter, Director, HR and Administration, Kawasaki Motors Corp., USA**

"This book helps leaders reflect on what keeps them going and help others feel comfortable doing the same. It is critical to make what Susan writes in her book into a habit."

—**Marios Loucaides, CEO, Cyprus Trading Corporation Plc, Nicosia, Cyprus**

"No motivational buttons, no inspiring speeches, no carrots, and no sticks; instead, Susan proposes developing a greater awareness of ourselves, practicing mindfulness, and learning to align values and purpose. We should listen instead of talking and search for the right questions instead of the right answers."

—**Marius Tanase, Executive Director, Farmexpert**

"Some ideas are way ahead of their time; Optimal Motivation is one of them and will shock you out of old methods of motivating people. It is the most revolutionary theory of motivation in decades."

—**Andrei Foisor, Country Manager, Roche Diabetes Care, Romania**

"Susan's book is provocative and pragmatic at the same time. She has successfully tapped into a longing I have had as a leader: how can I help people do what I think they naturally want to do—grow, develop, and fulfill their potential? Susan's propositions are surefire and easy to put into action."

—**Dr. Santrupt B. Misra, CEO, Carbon Black Business, and Director, Group Human Resources, Aditya Birla Group**

Why
Motivating
People
Doesn't Work ...
and What Does

Why Motivating People Doesn't Work... and What Does

The New Science of Leading, Energizing, and Engaging

Susan Fowler

BK

Berrett–Koehler Publishers, Inc.
San Francisco
a BK Business book

Berrett-Koehler Publishers, Inc., 1333 Broadway, Suite 1000,
Oakland, CA 94612-1921 Tel: (510) 817-2277   Fax: (510) 817-2278
www.bkconnection.com

Ordering Information
Quantity sales. Special discounts are available on quantity purchases by
corporations, associations, and others. For details, contact the "Special Sales
Department" at the Berrett-Koehler address above.
Individual sales. Berrett-Koehler publications are available through most
bookstores. They can also be ordered directly from Berrett-Koehler:
Tel: (800) 929-2929; Fax: (802) 864-7626; www.bkconnection.com
Orders for college textbook/course adoption use. Please contact
Berrett-Koehler: Tel: (800) 929-2929; Fax: (802) 864-7626.
Orders by U.S. trade bookstores and wholesalers. Please contact Ingram
Publisher Services: Tel: (800) 509-4887; Fax: (800) 838-1149; E-mail:
customer.service@ingrampublisherservices.com; or visit www.ingram
publisherservices.com/Ordering for details about electronic ordering.

Library of Congress Cataloging-in-Publication Data
Fowler, Susan, 1951–
   Why motivating people doesn't work . . . and what does : the new science
of leading, energizing, and engaging / Susan Fowler.
    pages cm
ISBN 978-1-62656-182-3 (hardback)
ISBN 978-1-62656-945-4 (paperback)
1. Employee motivation. 2.Leadership. I. Title.
HF5549.5.M63F69 2014
658.3'14—dc 23   2014021154

FIRST EDITION
21 20 19 18 17   10 9 8 7 6 5 4 3 2

Interior Illustration by Gary Onstad
Book design and production by Beverly Butterfield
Author photo by Ryan Talbot
Copyediting by PeopleSpeak
Indexing by Rachel Rice

For Drea

• Contents

• Foreword by Ken Blanchard

I am a fan of cutting-edge leadership. Over thirty years ago, we introduced Situational Leadership II (SLII), which revolutionized the way managers lead. In this book, Susan Fowler introduces the Spectrum of Motivation, a model that will revolutionize the way leaders think about motivation and evolve their leadership.

I am proud of the quality of thinking in this book. Susan has pursued the study and application of motivation science for almost twenty years. Together with David Facer and Drea Zigarmi, she developed the innovative Optimal Motivation training experience with the Ken Blanchard Companies and then field-tested it with trailblazing leaders and thousands of people from business, government, and nonprofit organizations around the world. What really excites me are the real-world stories and examples that show how this groundbreaking approach to motivation works.

I think you will be as excited about these ideas as I am, so I need to warn you about something we learned years ago. In the early years of teaching SLII, leaders would leave the training session eager to put their new skills to work. We were surprised by how they immediately applied the concepts without conversations with their employees to explain what they were doing. They followed the SLII model, backing off on direction and support for the self-reliant achiever, leaving her alone to do her thing. They provided direction and close supervision to an employee who was an inexperienced enthusiastic beginner. But when the two employees got together in the lunchroom, the experienced employee commented on how she had not seen her manager for weeks. The inexperienced employee said, "No wonder—he's constantly in my office. I don't know what I did wrong."

We learned over the years to remind leaders that *leadership is not something you do to people; it is something you do with people.* I am fascinated how the ideas Susan writes about in this book and SLII complement one another. One model, the Spectrum of Motivation, is on the cutting edge of new science—the other is now the most used management model in the world. Both models provide leaders with specific actions and language for helping people grow, learn, produce, and thrive. They both require conversation and direct communication with the individuals you lead.

I am both amused and saddened when leaders tell me they don't have time to have meaningful conversations with their people. It makes me wonder what being a leader means to them. I'll catch you on the back end of the book in the afterword with the hope that between now and then you might reconsider what leadership means to you—and the people you lead.

• Introduction:
Stop Beating Your People with Carrots

Are you motivated to read this book? You might find this a
silly question given that you are reading it. I agree it is silly
but perhaps for a different reason.

Asking if you are motivated raises more questions than
answers. What criteria do you use to determine if you are
motivated? If I asked you to decide if a colleague of yours
is motivated to read this book, how would you reach your
conclusion? How do you evaluate another person's motivation? What does *motivation* even mean?

For many years, my go-to definition of motivation was
simply "the energy to act." It turns out my definition has
the same fatal flaw as the other 102 definitions you can
find for motivation.[1] Thinking of motivation as having the
energy or impetus to act fails to convey the essential nature
of human motivation. It does nothing to help you understand the reasons behind the action.

Ask the Right Question

Back to my opening question. Are you motivated to read
this book? This is simply the wrong question. What if I
asked instead, Why are you motivated to read this book?
I might discover that the reason you are reading the book
is because you take being a leader seriously and you are

struggling with the motivation of a member of your staff. You are hoping this book might shed light on your motivation dilemma. Or I might discover that you are reading this book because the head of your department told you to read it and you're afraid of what might happen if you don't. These are two very different reasons for being motivated that generate different qualities of energy. Instead of asking if you are motivated, I need to ask a different question to reveal your *reasons* for acting.

An important truth emerges when we explore the nature of motivation. *People are always motivated.* The question is not *if*, but *why* they are motivated.

The motivation—or energy and impetus—a person brings to any action can be *qualitatively* different. Some reasons people are motivated tend to promote well-being for themselves and others—and unfortunately, some reasons don't.

- Motivation that comes from *choosing* to do something is different from motivation that comes from *having* to do it.

- Motivation generated from values, purpose, love, joy, or compassion is different from motivation generated from ego, power, status, or a desire for external rewards.

- Motivation to compete because of a desire to excel (where the score serves as feedback on how successfully you are growing, learning, and executing) is different from competing for the sake of besting someone else, to impress, or to gain favors.

One of the primary reasons motivating people doesn't work is our naïve assumption that motivation is something a person has or doesn't have. This leads to the erroneous conclusion that the more motivation a person has, the more likely she will achieve her goals and be successful. When it comes to motivation, assuming that more is better, is too simplistic and even unwise. As with friends, it isn't how many friends you have; it is the quality and types of friendships that matter.[2]

Imagine you are a sales manager. You wonder if your sales reps are motivated. You look at the midquarter sales reports for your two highest-selling reps and conclude, yes, they are both highly motivated. What you might fail to notice is that they are motivated differently. The reason one rep works hard is to win the sales contest, to be seen as number one, and to make the promised bonus. The reason the other rep works hard is because he values your products and services, his efforts are connected to a noble purpose, and he enjoys problem solving with his clients. The science of motivation provides compelling evidence that the reps' different types of motivation have major implications. The quality of their energy affects short-term results and long-term stamina.[3]

Traditional motivation prompts the questions, Is this person motivated? How much motivation does this person have? These questions reduce your answers to simplistic black-and-white, yes-or-no responses that fail to provide much-needed insight into the nature of the motivation. But asking *why* a person is motivated leads to a spectrum of motivational possibilities. Appreciating these possibilities, and the implications behind each of them, enables you to take advantage of the new science of motivation and guide your people to a more optimal and higher-quality motivational experience.

We Have Learned How to Put the Science to Work

My curiosity about motivation peaked in 1985, when virtually overnight I became a strict vegetarian. A study on how we treat animals so moved me that I simply could not eat animals anymore. People who knew how much I had enjoyed eating meat remarked on my amazing discipline. I found this intriguing. My new behavior had required no discipline at all. I found myself energized yet grounded in my new lifestyle. In almost thirty years, that dedication has not wavered.

I developed personal motivational theories about my experience, but it was not until I caught *The Oprah Winfrey Show* on October 14, 1996, that I began to understand the science behind my motivation. Winfrey's guest was Alfie Kohn, author of *Punished by Rewards—The Trouble with Gold Stars, Incentive Plans, A's, Praise, and Other Bribes.*[4] Winfrey announced that Kohn's message could be revolutionary, that it would change the way viewers think about parenting. Kohn's primary point was for parents and teachers to stop bribing children for doing things they are already inclined to do—such as learn, grow, and excel. Bribing children, Kohn asserted, killed the intrinsic motivation of the behavior being rewarded.

Kohn's ideas resonated with me—but I was not a parent or a teacher. Those who were, fought back. They were not just dismissive of the ideas—they were angry. Couldn't Mr. Kohn understand that when a child won't stop crying, ice cream can be your best friend? When a kid won't read, promising a prize prompts him to pick up the book. When your daughter doesn't do her chores, rewarding her does the trick. One mother stood by her tactics—she had doled out thousands of dollars to her kids. Bribes and incentives were the only way she could get them to listen to her.

Kohn tried to explain that rewards and punishments *can* work at the moment, but they only buy one thing: temporary compliance. Kohn tried to convey the undermining effect these carrot-and-stick tactics have on the quality of a child's learning, comprehension, and commitment—especially over time. He challenged parents and teachers to consider what happens when the reward or pressure is gone or resources run dry. Since the reward was the reason for action, the child will have no interest without the reward. Kohn pleaded, children should not be trained like pets.

Alas, Kohn's focus was on what parents and teachers needed to stop doing. You could see, hear, and feel their fear. *What does he expect of us? What should we do instead?* Kohn did his best, but under the glaring lights of national television and with limited time, his explanation of these cutting-edge ideas came off as defensive.

Now we have decades of data and uplifting research that undeniably demonstrate how alternative approaches to motivation make a difference. I now understand why becoming—and remaining—a vegetarian was so easy for me. I have been able to translate that knowledge and apply it to other tasks, goals, and situations in both my personal life and my professional life.

Through years of experience, we have learned how to position and promote the provocative research by Dr. Edward Deci, Dr. Richard Ryan, and other groundbreakers upon whose work Kohn and other popular writers such as

Daniel Pink have based their ideas. Thanks to these dedicated researchers, we have come to understand the true nature of human motivation. It is full of hope and promise.

The time is right to challenge antiquated ways of leading through a combination of contemporary motivation science and real-world application. There is a different and better way to approach motivation—which raises a question: *If there is a proven better way to approach motivation, why aren't more leaders using it?*

This question has three potential answers. Which of the three best describes you?

- You are not aware of the evidence.
- You don't believe the evidence.
- You don't know what to do with the evidence.

Potential answer 1: You are not aware of the evidence

A funny thing happened on the way to understanding human motivation. Psychologists decided to study animals. For example, you can watch Harvard psychology professor B. F. Skinner on YouTube showing how he "motivates" a conditioned pigeon to do a 360-degree turn by rewarding its behavior with pellets. It is fascinating to watch—he rewards the bird for doing what he wants it to do, and he can get it to do almost anything. Behaviorists reasoned that this method could motivate people in the workplace the same way: reward people for doing what you want them to do, and you can get them to do almost anything. And guess what? It worked—or seemed to. My colleagues and I call it the Pecking Pigeon Paradigm.

Using metaphorical pellets as incentives to "motivate" employees to do tasks they don't necessarily want to do has become common practice. A massive industry has evolved providing complex schemes to motivate workers with compensation systems, rewards, contests, tokens, badges, prizes, and formal recognition programs. Pellets and more pellets.

Current data clearly demonstrate the futility of the Pecking Pigeon Paradigm. In thousands of experiments worldwide, the results are the same: even though people will take the money or rewards you offer, the only correlation between those incentives and performance is a negative one. In other words, external rewards produce a disturbing undermining effect on the energy, vitality, and sense of positive well-being people need to achieve goals, attain excellence, and sustain effort.[5]

Traditional forms of motivation may appear to work in some types of jobs or industries. For example, if you promise people more pellets, they may produce more on the assembly line in the short term. However, it is unwise to confuse productivity with thriving and flourishing. Without thriving and flourishing, short-term gains tend to turn into long-term opportunity losses. The Pecking Pigeon Paradigm *never* worked the way we thought it would—no matter the type of job or industry. The simple fact is, *people are not pigeons.*

While this book provides relevant research to help you appreciate the compelling evidence showing how outdated modes of motivating people do not work, its focus is on

helping you develop the leadership skills to take advantage
of it.

Potential answer 2: You don't believe the evidence

Can you complete these statements?

- It's not personal; it's just _____.
- The purpose of business is to _____.
- Leaders are in a position of _____.
- The only thing that really matters is _____.
- If you cannot measure it, it _____.

These beliefs are so embedded in our collective psyche
that you probably don't even need to check your answers.
(But if you are curious, you can take a peek at chapter 6,
which is dedicated to exploring these beliefs.) Just because
these statements represent common beliefs doesn't mean
they are legitimate. I encourage you to consider that holding on to these beliefs may undermine your ability to effectively investigate alternatives, change your methods of
motivation, and embrace new ways of leading. Chapter 6,
"Rethinking Five Beliefs That Erode Workplace Motivation"
challenges you to reconsider your own beliefs about motivation, where they come from, and if they still serve you,
your people, and your outcomes.

Through the exploration of evidence and alternative approaches to motivation, I hope you will come to appreciate
how your basic beliefs may be undermining your leadership intentions. For example, your belief in driving for
results may be creating the psychological distress, tension,

and pressure that makes it less likely you'll get the quality short-term results or sustainable long-term outcomes that you—and those you lead—are seeking.

Potential answer 3: You don't know what to do with the evidence

You may be familiar with scientific evidence proving how traditional methods of motivation undermine employees quality of work and productivity.[6] It may have captured your imagination and piqued your curiosity. But as often happens in attempts to simplify science, the ideas get boiled down to clichés that make them difficult to use. For example, the virtues of intrinsic motivation resonate with most of us at a deep level. They also cause fear and trepidation as the leader within you wonders, *What are alternatives to abandoning the stick and weaning people off the carrot? How do I get and keep people intrinsically motivated?* As well-intentioned as these questions are, they still reflect a traditional approach to motivation that suggests motivation is something you do *to* people.

Popular books and speakers are doing the important job of raising awareness about the positive attributes of intrinsic motivation and the detrimental effects of extrinsic motivation. But the simplistic duality of good-bad, internal-external, either-or does not provide enough depth to use the ideas in a meaningful way.

Misunderstanding what motivation means leads to a misapplication of techniques to make it happen.

Admitting that many traditional approaches to motivation practiced all these years have been counterproductive—or worse, destructive—frees us up for new ways of looking at motivation. We need to realize that applying pressure to achieve results has undermined the results we were seeking. We need to consider that promoting competition or winning a contest is not the best way to encourage and sustain performance. We need to appreciate that—despite the practical need for money and people's incessant requests for more—the focus on monetary rewards has obscured what really satisfies people in their jobs. It appears motivating people doesn't work to generate the type of results we need. Leaders need alternatives that do. It is time to stop beating our people with carrots and sticks and embrace different, more effective, leadership strategies.

When it comes to motivation, we have underestimated ourselves—and perhaps even cheated ourselves—of something richer and much more meaningful than pellets, carrots, and sticks. By falling prey to the outdated Pecking Pigeon Paradigm, we convinced ourselves that this was the nature of motivation, and we bypassed the more human reasons we work.

The new science of motivation is full of promise. There are alternatives to the outdated Pecking Pigeon Paradigm and the constant grind to provide more and better pellets to get people to do what you want them to do. It shouldn't surprise you that people don't find those pigeons pellets satisfying.

From Theory to Practice

Motivating people doesn't work, but this book provides you with a framework, model, and powerful course of action that does. You will also discover a fresh and much-needed new vocabulary for thinking about and expressing motivation. Outdated terminology—such as *driving for results* or *incentivizing behavior*—leads you down the wrong path if you are looking for motivation that generates productivity without compromising positive and enduring energy, vitality, and well-being for the people you lead.

- Chapter 1, "The Motivation Dilemma," explains why motivating people does not work and introduces the Spectrum of Motivation model as an alternative.

- Chapter 2, "What Motivates People: The Real Story," reveals the true nature of human motivation, the benefits of tapping into it, and the hidden costs of continuing to ignore it.

- Chapter 3, "The Danger of Drive," presents alternatives to driving for results that, ironically, lead to better results.

- Chapter 4, "Motivation Is a Skill," provides a deeper appreciation of what individuals need for shifting the quality of their own motivational experience and the skill to help them do it.

- Chapter 5, "Making Shift Happen," teaches leaders how to conduct a motivational outlook conversation that facilitates a person's shift to higher-quality motivation.

- Chapter 6, "Rethinking Five Beliefs That Erode Workplace Motivation," confronts how your beliefs and values may undermine leadership practices and recommends best practices that support and encourage people's optimal motivation.

- Chapter 7, "The Promise of Optimal Motivation," examines the potential of this fresh approach to motivation from three perspectives: the organization, the leaders, and the people who long to flourish in the workplace.

This book is for leaders with the strength to question traditional beliefs and common practices. It is for leaders who recognize that outdated approaches to motivation compromise people's energy, creativity, well-being, and health—both mental and physical. This book is for leaders who want to cultivate a workplace where people flourish. This book is for you if you yearn for a practical yet honorable way to achieve and sustain results that also brings out the best in—and for—people.

The Motivation Dilemma

Imagine you have the perfect person in mind to recruit and hire as a new employee. Your offer includes the highest salary ever offered to someone in this role. You are authorized to include whatever it takes to motivate this person to work in your organization—signing bonus, moving allowance, transportation, housing, performance bonuses, and a high-status office.

This was the situation facing Larry Lucchino in 2002. His mission: lure Billy Beane, the general manager of the small-market Oakland A's, to the Boston Red Sox, one of the most storied and prestigious franchises in baseball. Lucchino was impressed with Billy's innovative ideas about using *sabermetrics*—a new statistical analysis for recruiting and developing players.

The Red Sox offered Billy what was at the time the highest salary for a GM in baseball's history. The team enticed him with private jets and other amazing incentives. As you may know from *Moneyball: The Art of Winning an Unfair Game* by Michael Lewis or from the hit movie starring Brad Pitt, Billy turned down the historic offer.

In real life, Billy is almost a shoe-in for the Baseball Hall of Fame because of the choices he has made, the relative success of the low-payroll Oakland A's, and how he revolutionized the game of baseball through sabermetrics. He also provides an example of what *you* face as a leader. The Boston Red Sox could not motivate Billy Beane to be the team's general manager with a huge paycheck and extravagant perks.

Billy's mom, Maril Adrian, is one of my dearest friends. It was fascinating to hear her perspective as Billy's life unfolded in the media over the decade. *Sports Illustrated* corroborated her assertion that money didn't motivate Billy: "After high school, Beane signed with the New York Mets based solely on money, and later regretted it. That played into his decision this time."[1]

To understand Billy's choices is to appreciate the true nature of human motivation and why motivating people doesn't work. Billy was motivated. He was just motivated differently than one might expect. He was not motivated by money, fame, or notoriety but by his love of and dedication to his family and the game of baseball. Trying to motivate Billy didn't work because he was already motivated. People are always motivated. The question is not *if* a person is motivated but *why*.

The motivation dilemma is that leaders are being held accountable to do something they cannot do—motivate others.

I was sharing these ideas with a group of managers in China when a man yelled, "Shocking! This is shocking!" We all jumped. It was really out of the ordinary for someone in a typically quiet and reserved audience to yell something out. I asked him, "Why is this so shocking?" He replied, "My whole career, I have been told that my job as a manager is to motivate my people. I have been held accountable for motivating my people. Now you tell me I cannot do it." "That's right," I told him. "So how does that make you feel?" "Shocked!" he repeated, before adding, "and relieved."

This led to a robust conversation and an epiphany for leaders and human resource managers in the room. They came to understand that their dependence on carrots and sticks to motivate people had become common practice because we didn't understand the true nature of human motivation. Now we do. Letting go of carrots and sticks was a challenge because managers did not have any alternatives. Now we do.

The Appraisal Process: How Motivation Happens

Understanding what works when it comes to motivation begins with a phenomenon every employee (and leader) experiences: the appraisal process.

Why do we say that people are already motivated?

Assuming that people lack motivation at any time is a mistake! For example, when you lead a team meeting, it's a mistake to assume that participants are unmotivated if they are checking their text messages or tweeting instead of paying attention to you. They may just not be motivated to be at the meeting for the same reasons you are. They have appraised the situation, come to their own conclusions, and gone in their own motivational direction.

To experience this appraisal process for yourself, think about a recent meeting you attended. Reflect on your different thoughts and emotions as you noticed the meeting on your calendar, jumped off a call, and rushed to make the meeting on time. Did your feelings, opinions, or attitudes fluctuate from the time you added the meeting to your schedule to the time you left the meeting burdened with all the "next steps" on your to-do list?

This reflection process is what your people are doing all the time—either consciously or subconsciously. They are appraising their work experience and coming to conclusions that result in their intentions to act—either positively or negatively.

The appraisal process in figure 1.1 captures what you might have experienced in the example of attending the meeting.[2] Whether mindful of it or not, you had thoughts and feelings about attending the meeting—you had both cognitive and emotional responses to the meeting. *Is the meeting a safe or threatening event? Am I feeling supported or threatened? Is it a good use of or a waste of my time? Am I excited or fearful? Am I attending because I want to or because I feel I have to?* Ultimately, how you *feel* about the meeting has the greatest influence on your sense of well-being. Your well-being determines your intentions, which ultimately lead to your behavior.

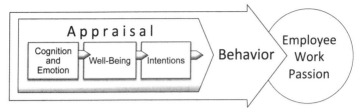

Figure 1.1 The appraisal process

Every day, your employees' appraisal of their work-place leaves them with or without a positive sense of well-being. Their well-being determines their intentions, and intentions are the greatest predictors of behavior.[3] A positive appraisal that results in a positive sense of well-being leads to positive intentions and behaviors that generate employee engagement.

The heart of employee engagement

The appraisal process is at the heart of employee engagement—and disengagement.[4] I would be surprised if your organization doesn't assess employee engagement or have some type of initiative aimed at improving it. Tons of data support the value of an engaged workforce. However, researchers have only recently explored *how* people come to be engaged.[5] How do you improve engagement scores if you don't understand the internal process individuals go through to become engaged?

You may find this encouraging: cutting-edge researchers discovered a higher level of engagement beyond the disengaged, actively disengaged, and engaged employee.

They call it *employee work passion*. An individual with employee work passion demonstrates these five positive intentions:[6]

- Performs above standard expectations
- Uses discretionary effort on behalf of the organization
- Endorses the organization and its leadership to others outside the organization
- Uses altruistic citizenship behaviors toward all stakeholders
- Stays with the organization

In these studies, researchers identified twelve organizational and job factors that influence a person's positive appraisal process.[7] When the factors are in place, people are more likely to experience a positive sense of well-being that leads to positive intentions and behavior. Over time, they experience employee work passion.

You can build an organization that supports employee work passion. You can change job designs, workload balance, distributive and procedural justice issues, and other systems and processes proven to encourage people's positive intentions. All of this is good news, but setting up new systems and processes takes time, and you need results *now*. What if you could help people manage their appraisal process today? *You can.*

This leads to a bold assertion: *Motivating people may not work, but you can help facilitate people's appraisal process so they are more likely to experience day-to-day optimal motivation.*

Optimal motivation means having the positive energy, vitality, and sense of well-being required to sustain the pursuit and achievement of meaningful goals while thriving and flourishing.[8]

This leads to a second bold assertion: *Motivation is a skill. People can learn to choose and create optimal motivational experiences anytime and anywhere.*

Before you can help your people navigate their appraisal process or teach them the skill of motivation, you need to master it yourself—and that leads back to your meeting experience.

A Spectrum of Motivation

Asking if you or your staff were motivated to attend a meeting is the wrong question. Your answer is limited to a yes-no or a-little–a-lot response rather than the quality of motivation being experienced. Asking *why* people were motivated to attend the meeting, however, leads to a spectrum of motivation possibilities represented as six motivational outlooks in the Spectrum of Motivation model, figure 1.2.[9]

The Spectrum of Motivation model helps us make sense of the meeting experience. Consider which of the six motivational outlooks, shown as bubbles, best describes your experience before, during, and after your meeting. These outlooks are not a continuum. You can be at any outlook at any time and pop up in another one at any time. In the meeting example, you may have experienced one or all of these outlooks at one point or another:

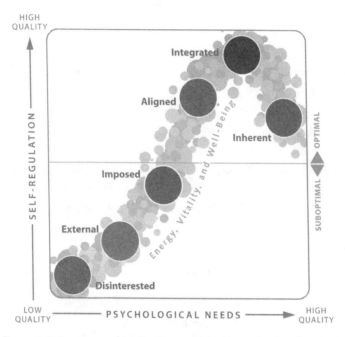

Figure 1.2 Spectrum of Motivation model—Six motivational outlooks

- *Disinterested motivational outlook*—You simply could not find any value in the meeting; it felt like a waste of time, adding to your sense of feeling overwhelmed.

- *External motivational outlook*—The meeting provided an opportunity for you to exert your position or power; it enabled you to take advantage of a promise for more money or an enhanced status or image in the eyes of others.

- *Imposed motivational outlook*—You felt pressured because everyone else was attending and expected the same from you; you were avoiding feelings of guilt, shame, or fear from not participating.

- *Aligned motivational outlook*—You were able to link the meeting to a significant value, such as learning—what you might learn or what others might learn from you.

- *Integrated motivational outlook*—You were able to link the meeting to a life or work purpose, such as giving voice to an important issue in the meeting.

- *Inherent motivational outlook*—You simply enjoy meetings and thought it would be fun.

You may have noticed on the Spectrum of Motivation model that three of the outlooks are labeled as *suboptimal*—disinterested, external, and imposed. These outlooks are considered motivational junk food, reflecting low-quality motivation. Three of the outlooks are labeled as *optimal*—aligned, integrated, and inherent. These outlooks are considered motivational health food, reflecting high-quality motivation. To take full advantage of the Spectrum of Motivation, it is important to appreciate the different effects suboptimal and optimal motivational outlooks have on people's well-being, short-term productivity, and long-term performance.

The Problem with Feeding People Motivational Junk Food

You buy dinner for your family at the local drive-through—burgers, fries, and shakes—with the intention of eating it at home together. The aroma of those fries is intoxicating. You simply cannot help yourself—you eat one. By the time you get home, the bag of French fries is empty.

Consider the effect junk food has on our physical and mental energy. How do we feel after downing the package of French fries? Guilty or remorseful? Even if we feel grateful and satisfied, what happens to our physical energy? It spikes dramatically and falls just as dramatically. How nourished are our bodies? A steady diet of junk food simply isn't good for us. Even if we can justify an occasional splurge, we are wise to understand our alternative choices.

Parents, teachers, and managers promise more money, award prizes for contests, offer rewards, threaten punishment, apply pressure, and use guilt, shame, or emotional blackmail to encourage specific behaviors from children, students, and employees. When people give in to one of these tactics, they end up with a suboptimal motivational outlook—disinterested, external, or imposed. But, those rewards and punishments (carrots and sticks) are as hard to resist as those French fries—and just as risky.

Here's a case in point. You receive an invitation from your health insurance provider to lose weight and win an iPad mini. You think, *What do I have to lose except some weight? What do I have to gain except health and an iPad mini?* Think again.

A recent study followed people who entered contests promising a prize for losing weight. They found that, indeed, many people lost weight and won their prize. However, these researchers did something that others had not done. They continued to follow the behaviors and results of the prizewinners. What they found reinforced vast motivational research findings regarding incentives. Within twelve weeks after winning their prize, people resumed old behaviors, regained the weight they had lost, and then added even more weight! Financial incentives do not sustain changes in personal health behaviors—in fact, they undermine those behaviors over time.[10]

Rewards may help people initiate new and healthy behaviors, but they fail miserably in helping people maintain their progress or sustain results. What may be more disturbing is that people are so discouraged, disillusioned, and debilitated by their failure, they are less likely to engage in further weight-loss attempts.

So why do over 70 percent of wellness programs in the United States use financial incentives to encourage healthy behavior changes?[11]

- If people participate, without perceived pressure, in a weight-loss program offering small financial incentives, there is some likelihood they will lose weight initially. However, studies reporting these weight-loss successes were conducted only during the period of the contest. They didn't track maintenance. "The rest of the story" is one that most people have not heard.

- Financial incentives are easy (if expensive to offer). Organizations have not taken the time to create more innovative, healthy, and sustainable options.

- People have come to feel entitled to receive incentives, and organizations are afraid to take them away.

Why do leaders keep promoting junk-food motivation to entice people to achieve goals or adopt certain behaviors?

- Many leaders simply don't question common practices.

- Leaders have not gained an awareness of the skill to ap ply the science of motivation to facilitate people's shift to a more optimal and sustainable motivational outlook.

- People don't understand the nature of their own motivation, so when they are unhappy at work, they ask for more money. They yearn for something different—but they don't know what it is—so they ask for the most obvious incentive: money. Managers take the easy way out and assume that since they can't comply with people's requests for more money, their hands are tied.[12]

Try Serving Motivational Health Food

Kacey is perennially a top salesperson in her organization. When her company announced a contest to award top sellers with a weeklong spa trip, she felt offended. "Do they think I do what I do so I can win a week at a spa? Maybe it sounds corny, but I work hard because I love what I do. I get great satisfaction by solving my clients' problems and seeing the difference it makes. If my company wants to connect with me and show appreciation—that's different. Obviously, that isn't the case. If they knew me, they would understand that as a single mother, a spa week away is not a reward but an imposition."

People with high-quality motivation, such as Kacey, may accept external rewards when offered, but this is clearly *not the reason* for their efforts. The reasons the Kaceys of the world do what they do are more profound and provide more satisfaction than external rewards can deliver.

Kacey would have found it easier if her organization had been more attuned to her needs rather than falling into the junk-food belief that salespeople are motivated by money and rewards. Instead, she found herself in an awkward situation. She didn't want to get sucked into the low-quality motivation of the reward trip, but she was fearful of offending her manager and colleagues by refusing the trip or complaining about the choice of reward.

Being an exemplary self leader, Kacey initiated a meeting with her manager to discuss the situation. She explained how the incentive program had the opposite effect than her manager had probably intended. She declared that she would continue selling and servicing her customers with her customary high standards—regardless of winning a reward. Kacey and her manager both described the conversation as "liberating." They felt it deepened their relationship because the manager now understood Kacey's internal dedication to her work.

At the end of the next sales cycle, Kacey had exceeded her goals for her own high-quality reasons. Instead of imposing a reward on her, Kacey's manager conferred with her about a way that he could express his gratitude for her achievements within fair price and time boundaries. Kacey chose an activity that she and her young child could enjoy together. Rather than interpreting the reward trip as a carrot to work harder, Kacey internalized it as an expression of her organization's gratitude. She reported how different the experience was from previous award trips: "The week took on special significance as a heartfelt thank-you from my manager and a wonderful memory-making experience with my child."

Kacey's deepened relationship with her manager and feeling valued was far more rewarding than winning a contest. There are significant implications for the organization when people experience high-quality motivation. They achieve above-standard results; demonstrate enhanced creativity, collaboration, and productivity; are more likely to repeat their peak performance; and enjoy greater physical and mental health.[13]

Junk Food or Health Food—You Choose

The three suboptimal motivational outlooks—disinterested, external, and imposed—are the junk foods of motivation. Their tangible or intangible rewards can be enticing in the moment, but they do not lead to flourishing. Far from it. People with a suboptimal motivational outlook are less likely to have the energy it takes to achieve their goals. But even if they do, they are not likely to experience the positive energy, vitality, or sense of well-being required to sustain their performance over time.[14]

The three optimal motivational outlooks—aligned, integrated, and inherent—are the health foods of motivation. They may require more thought and preparation, but they generate high-quality energy, vitality, and positive well-being that leads to sustainable results.

Motivation Mini Case Study: Himesh's Story

On his first day back at a plant in India after an Optimal Motivation training session, Himesh encountered one of his employees with a type of low-quality motivation. This technical service executive was in the lab having a discussion with an external contractor. Himesh noticed that the technician was wearing safety glasses, but she had not followed plant procedures to ensure the contractor was also protected.

Himesh is a strict manager with a no-tolerance policy when it comes to breaking safety regulations. His normal response to this flagrant breach of policy would be to call the technician to his office and, in his words, "read her the riot act." By the way, this is why Himesh had been in the training class. His plant's engagement scores were among the lowest in a global company that has more than fifty thousand employees.

According to Himesh's self-assessment, "I am known to blow a fuse (or two) when safety rules are flouted; however, I managed to keep my cool and decided to test my training." He asked the technician to come to his office. He could see that she was worried about his reaction. Instead of leading with his dismay and disappointment, Himesh started by explaining that he had just received some training on motivation. He shared key concepts with her. He then asked her if she thought that the rule to wear safety glasses, even when there was no experiment going on was stupid, as there is no danger to the eyes. Did she feel imposed upon by having to wear safety glasses at all times?

Since Himesh had invited the technician to have a discussion rather than a dressing down, she was open and candid. She explained that she had a two-year-old child and was extremely concerned about lab safety, as she wanted to reach home safe every evening. To Himesh's great surprise, she also shared that in certain areas, she would prefer even more stringent safety measures, not less stringent. For example, she suggested that safety shoes should be required for lab experiments conducted at elevated temperatures. But when no experiments were being conducted, she just could not understand the rationale for wearing safety glasses. Indeed, the technician expressed her resentment about the imposed rule. She wasn't compelled to enforce it, especially with an external contractor. Himesh listened and genuinely acknowledged her feelings. He then provided his rationale behind the regulation, explaining his hope and intention that wearing glasses would become a habit that protects people's lives, just like wearing a safety belt in the car.

Himesh said, "I saw the light dawn in her eyes."

It is important to note that Himesh did not attempt to motivate the technician. He recognized that she was already motivated—she was motivated not to follow the regulation. He challenged his natural tendencies, taking time to explore why she was motivated the way she was. By understanding the nature of her motivation, he had more options on how to lead: "I am sure if I had followed my normal instincts and given her a piece of my mind, I would have been met with a hangdog look, profuse apologies, and a promise to never do this again. And it probably would have happened again.

She would have gone away from my office with feelings of resentment and being imposed upon, and I would also have had a disturbed day due to all the negative energy."

Himesh's approach worked to shift his technician's motivation from low quality (imposed outlook) to higher quality (aligned outlook). Throughout this book we will explore some of the more subtle but powerful aspects of Himesh's motivational approach. As he reported, "Suffice it to say that in my view, my little experiment was a success. I have since shared what I learned with many of my team members and plan to have more motivational outlook conversations with them in the coming weeks."

Recapping "The Motivation Dilemma"

Motivating people does not work because they are already motivated—they are always motivated. The motivation dilemma is that even though motivating people doesn't work, leaders are held accountable for doing it. This dilemma has led to ineffective motivational leadership practices. You push for results, only to discover that pressure, tension, and external drives prevent people from attaining those results. Adding insult to injury, traditional motivational tactics focus on obtaining short-term results that tend to destroy long-term prospects.

Motivating people doesn't work, but what does work is further revealed in the next chapter. You will learn how to begin weaning people off motivational junk food and offer them healthy alternatives that will prove to be the key to your motivation dilemma.

2.

What Motivates People:
The Real Story

Have you ever thought about why you get out of bed in the morning (and stay up)? Why do you jump up enthusiastically on some mornings and drag yourself out of bed on others?

Have you ever wondered what it takes to walk away from the five-hundred-calorie muffin instead of caving in to the temptation?

Have you ever considered how your angry, defensive, or self-righteous energy differs from your loving, compassionate, and joyful energy?

Answers to these questions can be found in the compelling evidence that human beings have an innate tendency and desire to thrive. We want to grow, develop, and be fully functioning. Of course, the science is just catching up to what creative and thoughtful people have understood throughout our existence. Movies such as *The Wizard of Oz*, *Star Wars*, and *Gravity* portray our nature to thrive. Poets such as Kahlil Gibran, Maya Angelou, and Robert Frost have reflected our longing for wholeness. Ancient and modern artists and musicians continue to capture our yearning for self-identity, growth, and a meaningful connection to others. We want to flourish—but we cannot do it alone. We are, by nature, social animals. Striving to reach our individual human potential is natural, yet we innately recognize that the interconnection between ourselves and the world around us is a vital part of that process.

Our desire to thrive may be innate, but thriving doesn't happen automatically—especially at work. Just because we gravitate toward psychological growth and integration doesn't guarantee it will happen. Human thriving in the workplace is a dynamic potential that requires nurturing. The workplace either facilitates, fosters, and enables our flourishing or it disrupts, thwarts, and impedes it. In fact, conventional motivational practices have undermined more often than they've encouraged our human potential.

The bad news is that we have paid a high price for working with outdated ideas about motivation. The good news is that this is where the new science of motivation emerges as both a radical departure and an exciting opportunity.

If you come to know the real story of motivation, you will experience a shift in the way you live and work—and, importantly, in the way you lead.

Illuminating the True Nature of Human Motivation

The title of this book states that motivating people does not work. It also promises an answer to the question, What does work? The essence of the answer lies at the heart of the science of motivation and the revelation of three psychological needs—*autonomy, relatedness, and competence*. Regardless of gender, race, culture, or generation, the real story behind our motivation is as simple and as complex as whether or not our psychological needs are satisfied.

You will note that I use the terms *autonomy, relatedness,* and *competence* when exploring the individual attributes of these needs and ARC when pointing out their collective power—which is substantial.

If you need confirmation that these three psychological needs are essential to our thriving and flourishing, you can delve into the plentiful evidence provided by research over the past sixty years—much of it referenced throughout this book and listed in the notes, bibliography, and resource sections. You can consider the anecdotal evidence found in the stories, examples, and mini case studies generated from my experience in more than fifty countries over the past twenty years. You can also simply observe babies or recollect your own experience with toddlers. As you will discover in the next three sections, you can witness our psychological needs for autonomy, relatedness, and competence playing out from the moment we are born.

The First Psychological Need: Autonomy

Researchers have studied our need for autonomy and the effects of *not* having it more than any other psychological need.

Autonomy is our human need to perceive we have choices. It is our need to feel that what we are doing is of our own volition. It is our perception that we are the source of our actions.

A good example of autonomy is what happens when you feed a baby. What does the baby do as you bring a spoonful of baby food to his mouth? He grabs for the spoon—he wants to do it himself. He wants to be the source of that food going into his mouth. Despite not having the skill to feed himself, he has a need to control the situation.[1] If he is restrained by a high chair, he will shut his mouth or turn his head. This explains the orange smear of mashed carrots across the faces of babies in most mealtime photos.

If you are of a certain age, you will remember the animated Maypo cereal commercials. If not, search the Internet and watch these classics on YouTube. In one of my favorites, a father is trying to get his child to eat the maple-flavored oat cereal. The kid will have nothing of it. The father plays games with the spoon, hoping to entice his child to eat his Maypo, but as soon as the spoon comes near the kid's mouth, he clamps his mouth shut. Finally, the father appeals to the little boy's love of cowboys and pretends to be a cowboy taking a bite of the cereal. After one bite, the father realizes he loves the cereal and starts chowing it down himself. The kid sees his dad enjoying and eating all his cereal and cries out, "I want my Maypo!" Any parent who has engaged in reverse psychology is appealing to a child's need for autonomy. (Beware, however, that those tactics are likely to backfire. Children can detect manipulation a mile away. If they feel you are manipulating them, their second psychological need, relatedness, is undermined.)

Diverse studies over the past twenty years indicate that adults never lose their psychological need for autonomy.[2] For example, productivity increases significantly for blue-collar workers in manufacturing plants when they are given the ability to stop the line. So does the productivity of white-collar workers in major investment banking firms who report a high sense of autonomy. Employees experience autonomy when they feel some control and choice about the work they do. Autonomy doesn't mean that managers are permissive or hands-off but rather that employees feel they have influence in the workplace. Empowerment may often be considered a cliché, but if people don't have a sense of empowerment, their sense of autonomy suffers and so do their productivity and performance.[3]

It is a challenge for some people to grasp that everything they do is their own choice. Whether they are formally empowered or not, people can choose their own level of autonomy.

One of the most powerful examples of choosing autonomy is the description by psychologist Dr. Viktor Frankl of how he and others managed to survive in some of the worst conditions one can imagine—a World War II concentration camp. Frankl obviously had no freedoms accorded to him, yet he found ways to satisfy his basic need for autonomy by appreciating a beautiful sunrise, helping others who were suffering more than he was, and taking responsibility for his own frame of mind. Of that experience, he wrote, "Everything can be taken from a man but one thing; the last of the human freedoms—to choose one's attitude in any given set of circumstances, to choose one's own way."[4]

A workplace axiom says that autonomy is 20 percent given and 80 percent taken, so it is hard to make the case that we have the freedom to do what we want at work. However, the truth is, we have a choice to get out of bed, go to work, and make a contribution—or not. Anytime we take the position of not having a choice, we are undermining our experience of autonomy.

"If You Want to Motivate Someone, Shut Up Already"—I was curious about an article with this provocative title.[5] To find out more, I called Brandon Irwin, the lead researcher cited in the article, which highlighted motivational practices that don't work the way we thought. Brandon explained that initially his team was surprised to learn that when a sports or training coach is vocal, verbally encouraging a trainee—"do one more; come on, you can do it; keep up the energy"—performance is significantly lower than the results achieved with a quiet but attentive coach.[6]

Brandon hypothesizes that in light of what we know about autonomy, quiet coaches get better results than verbal coaches do because the verbal encouragement externalizes the exercisers' attention and energy. The shift from internal to external blocks the exercisers' sense of autonomy. The external encouragement and praising subverted the coaching subjects' own internal desire to perform, push, and excel—and thus limited their capacity to do so.

In an attempt to offset the distraction of the verbally encouraging coach, Brandon and his team tried incentives. If exercisers achieved a challenging goal (in spite of the verbal coaching), they would receive a prize such as a free gym membership. Consistent with studies showing how rewards tend to diminish performance in the short and long term, the added distraction of an external incentive—more motivational junk food—further blocked the exercisers' perception of autonomy, impaired their ability to tap into their own internal resources, and lowered performance even more.[7]

Brandon's results on vocal sports coaches also have interesting implications for the second psychological need—relatedness.

The Second Psychological Need: Relatedness

What does a toddler do when she is talking to you and you aren't looking at her? She grabs your face in her tiny hands and turns it in her direction, forcing you to look her in the eyes. Even in societies where it is not appropriate for someone of a lesser status to look someone of a higher status in the eye, children do it anyway—it is their natural response for connecting. No matter our age, social station, or culture, relatedness is one of our three psychological needs.

Relatedness is our need to care about and be cared about by others. It is our need to feel connected to others without concerns about ulterior motives. It is our need to feel that we are contributing to something greater than ourselves.

Notice the range of needs that relatedness covers. It is personal, interpersonal, and social. We thrive on connection.[8]

Several years ago, a worldwide electronics giant hired me to deliver a keynote in London to one hundred of its top global leaders. As I was about to go on stage, my host gave me a heads-up. I was the only thing standing between these one hundred leaders and their trip home after a weeklong conference. She explained that they were spent and might be restless during my ninety-minute speech. My host also apologized for their multitasking culture. She told me that speakers had complained all week about the lack of attention and the constant texting and e-mailing.

My host's warnings sparked my competitive nature—I would show them! I would be so compelling that they would forget about going home, cease their multitasking, and sit with rapt attention. About three minutes into my presentation, I was humbled. I did not have one person's eye contact. I could have been talking to a wall. I *was* talking to a wall—and it made me sad. Spontaneously, I made a decision to do something I had heard tales of from fellow speakers but, given my extraverted nature, had never dared to do. I shut up and just stood there—waiting, waiting, waiting—until the silence captured the audience's attention and I had every eye in the room staring at me curiously.

After what felt like an eternity, I slowly and quietly asked, "What is going on here? For some reason, your organization thought it was worth thousands of dollars to fly me thousands of miles to talk to you about these ideas that might make a difference in the way you lead. Obviously you don't agree. I'll make you a deal. Give me fifteen minutes. That is all I ask—fifteen minutes. If I cannot say something of value to you in fifteen minutes, I do not deserve your attention and you can go back to your cell phones, tablets, and computers."

They were now staring in disbelief. I had them—except for one young man who promptly returned to his keyboard and in a loud voice exclaimed, "Well, I can multitask, can't I?" I moved as close as I could before responding, fully tongue-in-cheek. "You could if you were a woman." The group broke out in laughter. Evidently, I had chosen the right guy to pick on. He looked up, smiled, and said, "Okay, hit me with your best stuff."

But instead of throwing my "stuff" at them, I abandoned the speech I had planned and led the group in a heartfelt discussion about what had just happened. It turned into one of those magical moments where we all learned something. I shared how I felt trying to do a good job and convey the ideas I was passionate about without their attention or any visible signs of appreciation from them. They talked about their fear of letting go of their electronic devices and not being in constant contact with people. It was interesting to explore how none of us had been getting our basic psychological need for relatedness satisfied.

One of their big aha moments was realizing how few of them—or the people they lead—were getting their relatedness needs met through work. Their employees' desire to be in constant contact with friends *outside of work* was due to their lack of relatedness *at work*—especially those in the Gen X or millennial generations.[9]

I ask you to consider the question I asked that group of global leaders: What percentage of your waking hours is spent connected to your work? Considering the time it takes getting ready for work, getting to work, working, getting home from work, and decompressing, you probably average 75 percent of your waking hours connected to your work. If your need for relatedness is not met at work and over 75 percent of your time is connected to work, then where *is* it being met? There is no such thing as *compensatory need satisfaction*. As leading researcher Dr. Jacques Forest told me, need satisfaction is important for everyone, all the time and everywhere. If you are not getting your needs for relatedness satisfied through your work, you are not likely to compensate for it in the limited amount of time you have outside of work.[10]

One of the great opportunities you have as a leader is to help your people find meaning, contribute to a social purpose, *and* experience healthy interpersonal relationships at work. The challenge is that exploring healthy interpersonal relationships in the workplace has been discouraged or even forbidden. Regrettably, beliefs such as "It's not personal; it's just business" diminish an aspect of work that is essential to our healthy functioning as human beings—the quality of our relationships.

When managers apply pressure to perform without regard to how it makes people feel, people interpret the managers' actions as self-serving. These too-common approaches to motivation undermine relatedness at work and people's performance.

The role you play as a leader is helping people experience relatedness at work: *caring about and feeling cared about, feeling connected without ulterior motives, and contributing to something greater than oneself.*

Dr. Brandon Irwin's study described in the section on autonomy showed that silent coaches garnered higher productivity from exercisers than verbally encouraging coaches did. It is important to note that having a coach mattered. People performed better with an exercise coach than without one. But you cannot deny the impact the *type of coaching* had. Brandon believes that relatedness also played a big part in the results.

The exercisers thought the verbal coaches were not acting in their best interest but were self-serving. In some cases, the exercisers interpreted the verbal pushing as the coach's need to win. In other cases, if exercisers perceived that the coach's ability to perform the goals he gave them was inferior to their own ability, they interpreted the verbal encouragement as being more for the sake of the coach's own motivation than for the motivation of the people he was coaching.

This finding is essential when it comes to interpersonal relationships at work. Your people will feel the opposite of relatedness if they think they're being used by you or the organization, sense that your attention is not genuine, or suspect they are simply a means to someone else's ends.

Motivating people doesn't work because you cannot force someone to feel a sense of relatedness. But as a leader, you can encourage relatedness by challenging beliefs and practices that undermine people's relatedness at work. That means paying attention to how your people feel. That means gaining the skill to deal with their emotions. That means getting personal.

The Third Psychological Need: Competence

Do you ever delight in watching babies learning to walk? What do you notice? They fall—a lot. You never question why they fall. It is obvious they are learning. But why do they get back up? When they pull themselves up to try again, why are they smiling and giggling instead of crying? The answer is that they find joy in learning, growing, and gaining mastery. Our third psychological need is competence.

Competence is our need to feel effective at meeting every-day challenges and opportunities. It is demonstrating skill over time. It is feeling a sense of growth and flourishing.

Anyone who has been around a two-year-old has experienced the toddler's incessant question, "Why?" Why does the toddler ask, why? Because she loves growing and learning. We encourage her learning by setting up systems to promote better learning, such as school. This is when we begin spurring her on with sticks in the form of stress to earn good grades and pressure to be at the top of her class and urge her to engage in activities that look good on college applications. We evaluate her learning, rewarding her positive performance with carrots in the form of gold stars, public praising, and student-of-the-month awards. Have you ever considered what happens to the 99.9 percent of the children who do not receive the rewards?

Some school systems started to see the futility of incentive programs set up to reward the few and discourage the many. Now the trend is "Everyone gets a trophy!" This solution does not provide the effective teaching or realistic feedback our children need for satisfying their competence.

Motivating children to learn won't work for the same reason that motivating adults doesn't work—they are already motivated to learn. Children have a psychological need to learn and grow. Bribing children with carrots or driving them with sticks diverts them from their natural love of learning. We question what happened to a child's sense of wonder as we watch him years later, just going through the motions of work. Children who succumbed to ineffective motivational techniques for learning and growing are now in the workplace hooked on motivational junk food in the form of pay-for-performance plans and elaborate reward and incentive programs.

Motivating people doesn't work because you can't impose growth and learning on a person. But you can promote a learning environment that doesn't undermine your people's sense of competence. What message do we send about the importance of competence when training is one of the first items cut in economically challenging times? What does it say about our belief in people's growth when educational opportunities focus on or are limited to managers and high-level executives? Ironically organizations will pull executives out of the office for multiday off-site strategy meetings but then fail to encourage ongoing training to enhance their leadership skills. Organizations are even less prone to provide training to improve rank-and-file employees' capacity to excel. Too bad. People need to have a sense of competence in every area of their lives—especially the place they spend most of their time. If they do not experience a sense of competence at work, there is a good chance they will not have a holistic sense of competence—and that will negatively affect every aspect of their lives.

At the end of each day, you may be missing a great opportunity if you only ask, "What did you achieve today?" Try adding, "What did you learn today? How did you grow?"

Psychological Needs: The Rainbow's ARC

Notice the connection between psychological needs and motivational outlooks. As you can see in the Spectrum of

Figure 2.1 Spectrum of Motivation model—Psychological needs

Motivation model, figure 2.1, when a person experiences high-quality psychological needs, she will have an optimal motivational outlook. In other words, if her needs for autonomy, relatedness, and competence are satisfied, the result is an aligned, integrated, or inherent motivational outlook. (In the color version of the Spectrum of Motivation model, these three optimal motivational outlooks are represented as high-frequency colors of the rainbow—blue, purple, and violet.)

When a person experiences low-quality psychological needs, he will have a suboptimal motivational outlook. In other words, if his autonomy, relatedness, and competence needs are not satisfied, the result is a disinterested, external, or imposed motivational outlook. (In the color version of the Spectrum of Motivation model, these three suboptimal motivational outlooks are represented as low-vibrating colors of the rainbow—red, orange, and green.)

The ARC Domino Effect

Even though I described each of the three psychological needs individually, appreciating the integrated nature of ARC is important.

Imagine you have a manager with control needs. She micromanages people and projects—whether they need it or not. She either fails to acknowledge or doesn't care about the opportunity loss she is creating through her inappropriate leadership style and its impact on the psychological needs of those she leads. She seems content with not changing her ways—after all, she has successfully moved up in the organization.

You have proven yourself to her over the years, especially when it comes to collecting sales data and submitting the quarterly report to headquarters. In fact, when she took a leave of absence, you completed the reports on your own. Yet your manager still demands to review and edit your reports and send them to headquarters herself. The changes she makes seem to be arbitrary. There is simply no pleasing her. Her micromanagement is undermining your sense of autonomy—she is controlling your work and not allowing you to think for yourself. You are afraid to go over her head to complain because you've seen what happens to complainers.

This is how the ARC Domino Effect begins. Your lack of autonomy raises questions in your mind about your competence. Your inability to manage your manager's over-involvement or the organizational politics involved further erodes your competence. Your manager's ineffective leadership, lack of sensitivity to your needs, and apparent self-interest prevent any sense of relatedness. Intangible external forces (her micromanaging style and your fear) dictate your internal sense of well-being. If the economy was better and jobs were easier to find, you would leave.

When it comes to your reports, you do them because you are afraid of what will happen if you don't. You have an imposed motivational outlook. Driven by fear, and maybe a little guilt, you do your job, all the while thinking, *I will do the reports because I have to, but I resent it. I will do just enough to get by.* You do not bother to think about the work creatively or add quality because your manager would probably change your work anyway.

Here comes more bad news. You begin to generalize your suboptimal motivational outlook by thinking, *The only reason I get up every day is to collect my paycheck!* Suddenly you have an external motivational outlook toward your job—it has become all about the money.

People revel in the positive energy, vitality, and sense of well-being that occur when all three psychological needs are satisfied. But—and this is a big but—one depends on the other. The ARC Domino Effect is in full force when even one psychological need is missing. If A or R or C falls, the others are diminished as well.

Motivation Mini Case Study: The Art of Schmoozing

As the food and beverage director at a midsize resort, Art was enjoying immediate success with his approach: "For waiters, it's all about the tips." He explained, "I teach my wait staff how to get better tips through schmoozing. They are motivated because the more they chat up customers, use their names, ooze charm, and even touch them appropriately, the higher their tips. They see a direct cause and effect."

This approach was working. Most of the wait staff were generating more tips. The question we need to consider is what motivational outlook Art's tactics encouraged. His focus on increased tips provided his wait staff with a sense of autonomy: *If I choose to schmooze, I'll get more tips.* Art's focus on specific behaviors and the immediate feedback of higher tips reinforced their success, growth, and learning— and probably a sense of competence.

While Art's approach seemed to satisfy his people's need for autonomy and competence, he was ignoring relatedness. In a people-oriented business, Art failed to encourage a connection between his wait staff and the people they were serving. Beyond earning more tips, few of his wait staff had a sense of meaning or deeper purpose to their work.

At the end of the night, a typical comment from a waiter reflected an external motivational outlook: "Wow, look at all the tips I made!" Consider the qualitative difference between that comment and one reflecting an optimal motivational outlook: "I think I may have been the only good thing that happened to that couple tonight. They came in grumpy but left laughing. It felt good to run interference for Tony when he got behind on two of his tables. We really were cranking as a team tonight—like a well-oiled machine. I had fun! I made a difference. And wow, on top of all that, I made money doing something I enjoy, am good at, and find meaningful."

Art missed a wonderful opportunity for creating a workplace where his staff could experience the power of ARC. He could have teed up success as building relationships, improving service, or establishing repeat customers rather than earning more tips. He could have helped his staff tap into their values for service, creativity in making improvements, or enjoyment of their job. He could have showed them how satisfaction comes from making a positive difference in a person's dining experience or from their own sense of enjoyment in the work. Art could have fostered a deeper, more significant experience for his staff by helping them shift from an external motivational outlook.

Not understanding what really motivates people came back to haunt Art. His focus on an external motivational outlook was simply not sustainable. When his staff had mastered schmoozing and maximized their tips, there was nowhere else to grow. When the season slowed down, the economy slumped, and there were fewer tips to be schmoozed out of people, his people's performance slowed and slumped as well.

When his staff, and the customers they served, started to complain, turnover increased. Art's response was, "The only way I can get people to improve their performance is to pay them more money, set up recognition programs, and reward and incentivize them to work harder. And I don't have the budget for that."

Art did what most organizations do when they don't have enough money to keep elevating pay and incentives to motivate people using traditional approaches to motivation—he pegged the role of waiter as a high turnover job. He tried to justify the increased costs of hiring and training as normal in the industry. He blamed incompetent people for the negative impact on sales and customer devotion.

Imagine if Art had understood what really motivates people. He could have encouraged autonomy, relatedness, and competence by providing more choices on how to succeed, helping the staff discover the meaning and value of serving others, and encouraging creativity and new skills. He could have generated more energy and vitality and sustained performance over the long run.

The irony was that the resort owners came to see Art as incompetent and let him go. They rationalized that the food and beverage director is a high turnover position.

Recapping "What Motivates People: The Real Story"

The real story of motivation is that people have psychological needs for autonomy, relatedness, and competence. It is a mistake to think that people are not motivated. They are simply longing for needs they cannot name. Do you know someone at work who wouldn't prefer to make good choices, be a positive force for good, or have a sense of wonder? I don't.

The real story of motivation is that people are learners who long to grow, enjoy their work, be productive, make positive contributions, and build lasting relationships. This is not because of motivational forces outside themselves but because it is their human nature. Chapter 3 explores why it is so challenging for people to satisfy needs that are essential to their own well-being.

3.

The Danger of Drive

Be careful of being driven. *If you are driven, who is doing the driving?* I heard this old adage many years ago, and ever since, being driven has held a negative connotation for me. I never liked the idea of something or someone outside of myself controlling me. However, it seems my interpretation is a minority opinion. Having a conversation about motivation in the English language without using the word *drive* is almost impossible. A person with a lot of drive is considered to have a lot of motivation. A person with low drive is considered not to have enough motivation. Inner drive is considered a good thing. On this last point, I could concede, but it depends on the nature of the inner drive. Where are you driving and why?

One of the most popular motivational theories of the past one hundred years is called Drive Theory. It made sense based on the idea that we are motivated to get what we don't have. If you are thirsty, you are driven to drink; if you are hungry, you are driven to eat. The pervasive use of Drive Theory paved the way to an acceptance of driving for results, driving for success, and driving performance. The problem with Drive Theory as a general theory of motivation is that after you drink or eat, your need is satiated and you are no longer driven to drink or eat until your body is deficient again. Now we are beginning to grasp the real costs of driving.

Anti-Drive Theory

Your psychological needs are not drives. In fact, they are just the opposite. Drives dissipate when they are satiated (such as thirst as we drink water or hunger as we eat food). However, when psychological needs are satisfied, you experience such positive energy, vitality, and a sense of well-being that you want more! You have probably experienced this with your own positive addictions, such as running, meditating, volunteering, playing with children, or being in the flow during an activity.

People who experience ARC are thriving. They do not need something or someone else doing the driving.

When Brandt, a student in a masters-level course on executive leadership at the University of San Diego where I teach, described himself as "intensely driven," I asked him a series of questions: Who or what is doing the driving? Are you driven by the promise of money, rewards, power, or status? Are you driven to dispel fear, shame, or guilt? Are you driven to avoid disappointing someone important or yourself?

Even though the nature of the weeklong course challenges high-level leaders to be introspective, I was impressed with Brandt's openness to investigating the source and quality of his drive. He shared that despite being a successful executive in a prestigious electronics company, he was longing for something he couldn't define. He felt out of balance physically, mentally, and emotionally. Brandt and I explored the underlying reasons for his intense work behavior, the gap between his espoused values and his lived values, and the difference between his reality and his dreams and life purpose. It didn't take long for Brandt to discover this reality: "Being driven" is another way of saying "I am not in control."

Brandt began to acknowledge that something external was driving him and prompting his emotions, feelings, and actions. That "something," it turned out, was his need to prove himself, fueled by a desire to impress his father—who happened to be a legend in the computer industry.

Finding that unexplored emotions and beliefs are at the root of dysfunctional behavior is not revolutionary. The revelation of *why* our sense of well-being, intentions, and behavior are dysfunctional is groundbreaking.

Dysfunction exists because our psychological needs for ARC are not being satisfied. Armed with understanding, we can do something about it.

It turns out that Brandt had been bouncing back and forth for years between an external motivational outlook—a craving for praise, validation, and tangible rewards, and an imposed motivational outlook—a fear of letting his father down. His drive to live up to self-imposed standards measured through promotions, financial success, and public recognition robbed him of his autonomy. Ironically, his desire to please his father prevented him from experiencing a true and authentic sense of relatedness. Brandt's competence always felt diminished in comparison to his perception of his father's competence. He had been searching for a way to ease his longings in all the wrong places and by all the wrong means.

Brandt's suboptimal motivational outlooks (external and imposed) were symptomatic of his low-quality of ARC and his negative energy, a lack of vitality, and a less-than-positive sense of well-being. He needed a way to break the vicious cycle of junk-food remedies that perpetuated his undesirable situation. Brandt put it perfectly when he said, "I have been eating way too many French Fries."

Self-Regulation: The Means to a Satisfying End

People *want* to thrive. People thrive when they experience autonomy, relatedness, and competence needs. So what's the problem?

Psychological needs are fragile.[1] Their power is in the combined potency of ARC—but if one is out of balance, the others are diminished. Workplace and life experiences can easily distract us from experiencing ARC. Organizations undermine our autonomy by tempting us with junk-food motivation. Individuals push emotional buttons that can destroy relatedness. The pace of change threatens our competence. How do we protect our psychological needs from all these distractions? The answer lies on the vertical axis of the Spectrum of Motivation model labeled self-regulation.[2]

Self-regulation is mindfully managing feelings, thoughts, values, and purpose for immediate and sustained positive effort.[3] You must understand the role self-regulation plays in helping you satisfy your own psychological needs. You

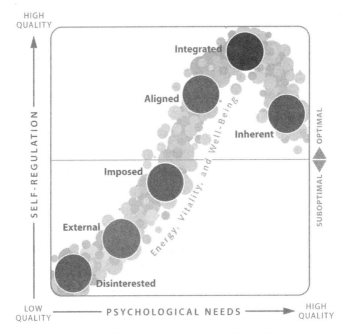

Figure 3.1 Spectrum of Motivation model—Self-regulation

must also appreciate your role in creating a workplace that fosters the high-quality self-regulation needed for your people to satisfy *their* psychological needs.[4]

The Nature of Self-Regulation: Eating the Marshmallow

Put a marshmallow in front of a kid and ask him to wait for fifteen minutes before eating it. Then leave the room and watch what happens via hidden cameras. That's what researchers did at Stanford University in the late 1960s and early 1970s: they told children if they waited fifteen minutes to eat their one marshmallow, they would receive an additional one.[5] In the research footage, you can see the children's eyes light up at the prospect of two marshmallows! The purpose of the experiment was to measure the children's capacity for delayed gratification. What follows next is eye-opening—and hysterical.

Some children lasted mere seconds before popping the marshmallow in their mouths. Others tried to wait. The techniques kids used to keep themselves from eating the marshmallow were fascinating. They covered their eyes, pretended to sleep, and walked around the room. Some kids licked the marshmallow to a puddle but refused to chew it. Some kids sniffed it until they almost inhaled it.

Years later, researchers revisited the subjects and compared their delayed-gratification scores to current life measures including SAT scores, level of education, and body mass index. They found a striking correlation. The children who had been able to delay their gratification for the marshmallow the longest, those with the greatest degree of self-regulation, had higher life measure scores. Researchers postulated that children with a higher quality of self-regulation had a greater likelihood of later-life success.

The marshmallow studies made a great case for self-regulation as a crucial element of later success. However, as an advocate for self leadership, I had concerns that some might interpret the results to mean that self-regulation is something people are born with rather than something they choose or can develop. This is why research by the University of Rochester in 2012 captured my attention.[6] These researchers wondered what effect children's rational thought process played in their capacity to self-regulate. In the Rochester experiments, "teachers" set up an art project to explore *why* some children demonstrate higher-quality self-regulation than others.

Children were put into one of two scenarios—a reliable situation and an unreliable situation. Told they had a choice, the children could start their art project immediately with the materials at hand (a few old, used crayons in a glass jar) or they could wait for the teacher to get the big supply of art materials. All the children elected to wait for the good stuff. A moment later the teacher in the reliable situation returned with the big supply as promised; in the unreliable situation, she returned with an apology for not having the big supply after all.

In the videos of the experiments, the first thing you notice is the children's reactions when the supplies arrive and the profound disappointment when they don't. The letdown of not getting bigger and better supplies as promised made them less likely to engage enthusiastically in their art.

Although this was an interesting development, with implications that go beyond children and art projects and into the workplace, this is not what the Rochester researchers were studying. It really was still all about those marshmallows. As the children continued their art projects with hidden cameras still on, the teacher announced it was time for a snack. The children were given another choice: eat a marshmallow now or wait for the teacher to come back with two marshmallows.

Viewing the videos, you witness many of the same tactics used by kids in the original marshmallow studies. Again, the kids' eyes light up at the prospect of two marshmallows. One kid nibbles the bottom of the marshmallow and puts it back on the plate, hoping no one will notice. One little boy sits on the marshmallow—out of sight, out of mind? Eventually, all the children eat their marshmallow within fifteen minutes.

There was one telling difference in these marshmallow studies compared to the original. Children in the reliable group, those who had received their art supplies as promised, had four times longer delayed gratification times (twelve minutes on average) than the children who experienced the unreliable situation (three minutes on average). *The quality of the children's self-regulation significantly correlated to their environment and experience.*

Researchers concluded that when children are in an environment where long-term gain is rare, it makes sense for them to maximize their reward now. Children figure it is not worth the emotional labor to delay gratification if they do not trust that gratification will ever come. It makes more sense for them to act impulsively than to self-regulate and hope to receive a payoff. Obviously, the children in the reliable group had a different experience—and a different interpretation of their options. They trusted it was worth the wait, based on past experience.

All this marshmallow eating has significant implications in the workplace. Remember the appraisal process described in chapter 1? Employees are constantly appraising their workplace—evaluating if it is reliable or unreliable, safe or threatening, trustworthy or untrustworthy. An individual is much more likely to have high-quality self-regulation in a reliable, safe, and trusting work setting.

Leaders and organizations need to work harder at creating a workplace where people don't have to work so hard to self-regulate.[7] Unfortunately, even the best workplaces can disappoint us, engender bad feelings, promote vulnerabilities, and provoke emotions that drive our impulse to gobble junk food—whether marshmallows, pellets, or French fries—as fast as we can. People cannot count on the perfect workplace—they need to learn how to self-regulate. They need to learn how to drive, instead of being driven.

If satisfying our psychological needs is the end, then self-regulation is the means.

The MVPs of Self-Regulation

Self-regulation is the mechanism for countering the emotional triggers and distractions that tend to undermine our psychological needs. People need high-quality self-regulation to help manage their workplace experiences if they ever hope to have an optimal motivational outlook. Three potent techniques promote high-quality self-regulation—mindfulness, values, and purpose. These are the MVPs of self-regulation.

Mindfulness: The first MVP of self-regulation

Mindfulness is noticing—being aware and attuned to what is happening in the present moment without judgment or an automatic reaction. It is a state of being but is also a skill that requires development through practice and patience.

I don't happen to have what is called dispositional mindfulness. It has taken years for me to be more mindful; I find I need daily practice. Every human being has the capacity for mindfulness—some more than others. My dispositional nature is to be quick to judge and react. I get a rush from the self-righteous indignation that comes from knowing I am right and someone else is wrong. I generate a surge of energy when I think my anger is justified by unfair, unjust, or what I consider stupid people, organizations, or systems. In my case, when I am mindless, my dispositional response is an extroverted, direct, fight response. I get a rush of "fight" energy and find myself putting the other person down, sniping, and complaining aloud. Sometimes I lash out—attacking the person's character or behavior.

Others express mindless reactions differently. Some convey anger, frustration, or self-righteous indignation by yelling, ranting, or bullying and others by going silent, being passive-aggressive, or avoiding the person or situation that seems most responsible for thwarting their psychological needs.

When we are not mindful, we tend to react with typical behavior patterns—many of which we are born with or have acquired unconsciously through life experience—or uncontrolled emotions when we feel

- We are pressured or lack control over a person or situation (an absence of autonomy)

- A person or organization has disappointed us or let us down (an absence of relatedness)

- We don't have the ability to cope effectively with the person or situation (an absence of competence)

Mindfulness, however, provides a view of reality without the filters, self-centered thoughts, and historical conditioning that tint your outlook.

When people are not in control of their reactions, their lack of mindfulness reflects low-quality self-regulation. The result is one of the three suboptimal motivational outlooks:

- *Disinterested*—People disengage because they are overwhelmed but not thoughtfully or through conscious choice; they are unable to link the activity with values or anything meaningful.

- *External*—They revel in the power they exert, stimulated by their status over others or controlled by an external reward or incentive.

- *Imposed*—They feel they have no other choices and there is only one way of dealing with the situation.

Ironically, suboptimal energy can be addictive. It is also exhausting. The rush of adrenalin generated through self-righteous indignation, the heat of anger, the thrill of the kill in intense competition—they can all fuel a person like junk food. Whether the energy is expressed more inwardly through passive aggression and silent disengagement or more outwardly through frustration or impatience, consider this: the only way to sustain the negative energy is to continue being mad, infuriated, and disappointed in whoever or whatever sparked the negativity in the first place. Sustaining negative energy requires fueling negative energy. It is no way to live.

My wish for people as they explore mindfulness is to discover how suboptimal motivational outlook energy pales in comparison to the energy generated in an optimal motivational outlook.

Mindfulness and ARC are directly linked. The high-quality self-regulation that comes from mindfulness is highly relevant to a person's motivational outlook. Kirk Warren Brown, a leading mindfulness researcher, reports on how mindfulness links to a direct experience of psychological needs. In other words, when people are mindful, it is almost impossible for them *not* to experience ARC. The neuroscience of mindfulness is fascinating. Brain scans show that mindfulness and the experience of ARC activate the same part of your brain. The more mindful you are, the more likely you are to satisfy your psychological needs.[8]

My colleague David Facer and I have witnessed this outcome firsthand in our Optimal Motivation training sessions. Participants identify a task, goal, or situation where they have a suboptimal motivational outlook. A learning partner poses questions from our Psychological Needs Checklist to determine how ARC is being experienced. Almost all participants who have completed the checklist report the same phenomenon: halfway through the list of questions, they feel their motivational outlook shifting. It is remarkable to watch. The questions, posed in a nonthreatening way, enable participants to be mindfully aware and suddenly they realize, *I do have choices. I do have values connected to this goal. I do have the opportunity to fulfill my purpose in this situation.* Through mindfulness, we can experience our greatest opportunities for growth and freedom.

A space exists between what is happening to you and the way you react to it. Mindfulness is that space. This is where you can choose how to respond.

When a person is mindful, she experiences a heightened sense of *autonomy* because she is not controlled by her own potentially misconstrued and misaligned self-concept based on irrelevant past experiences. In this mindful state, a person is better able to experience *relatedness* because she can be genuinely concerned about another person without self-serving interpretations or prejudice. Mindfulness also enhances her *competence* because without the knee-jerk response, she has options for making more appropriate choices—she is better able to navigate and master whatever situation she finds herself in.

When people are mired in their prejudiced version of reality, they have fewer options for coping with that reality.

Values: The second MVP of self-regulation

Values are premeditated, cognitive standards of what a person considers good or bad, worse, better, or best. Values are enduring beliefs a person has chosen to accept as guidelines for how he works—and lives his life.

Values are at the heart of high-quality self-regulation, yet most individuals have not explored their own work-related values. I find this ironic. If you stop people in the hallway at work and ask them to list their organization's values, purpose, or mission statement, chances are they will come close. Today, promoting organizational values and purpose is an accepted business practice. This is a good thing. However, we cannot stop there. Individuals need to identify, develop, clarify, declare, and operationalize their own work-related values and purpose—and then determine how they align with the organization's values.[9]

Employees with clarified values are more likely to experience high-quality self-regulation despite inevitable workplace demands and challenges. But therein lies the problem. First, people need to *have* developed values! If values are mechanisms for change and good decision making, shouldn't all individuals in the organization have clarity about their own values—and how they align, or not, with the organization's?

A theme of this book is that motivating people doesn't work because they are *already* motivated; they are *always* motivated. What matters is the *quality* of their motivation. The same is true of values. People are *always* acting from their values; what matters is the *quality* of their values.

Developing workplace values for yourself and with your people is worth the investment of time. Linking developed values to a challenging task, goal, or situation activates a shift between a suboptimal motivational outlook and optimal motivational outlook.

A developed value is freely chosen from alternatives, with an understanding of the consequences of the alternatives. It is prized and cherished. It is acted upon over time.

An intriguing aspect of values is that developing them tends to be a mindful process that reflects not only what we need to flourish but what others need as well. Acting upon developed values helps us satisfy our psychological needs.

To guide your people's shift to an optimal motivational outlook, help them self-regulate by linking assigned tasks, goals, or projects to their developed values. For you to do that, your people need to have developed values—and to have you as a good role model.

Purpose: The third MVP of self-regulation

Purpose is a deep and meaningful reason for doing something. Purpose is acting with a noble intention—when your actions are infused with social significance.

As consultant and author Dr. Charles Garfield drove over the San Francisco–Oakland Bay Bridge on his way to work, he heard loud music coming from the tollbooth he was about to enter. He rolled down his window to pay his toll and found a dancing tollbooth operator. "I'm having a party," the operator declared. Dr. Garfield drove away more joyful than he did most mornings and realized he had just experienced a peak-performing tollbooth operator.

Intrigued, Dr. Garfield followed up and discovered that the young man's purpose in life was to be a dancer. His coworkers described their booths as "vertical coffins," but this young man saw it as a stage for performing and his job as an opportunity to dance. He developed a philosophy about his job, created an environment to support his vision, and happened to entertain those he served.[10] Research on peak performers confirms what you might suspect about people who attain high levels of success and sustain it over time. *Peak performers are not goal driven. Peak performers are values based and inspired by a noble purpose.*

The danger of drive is that it distracts people from what really makes them dance. People are more likely to meet or exceed expectations when they pursue goals within a context of a meaningful purpose. If, for some reason, the dancing tollbooth operator were failing to achieve his goals of collecting correct fees and preventing backups on the bridge, as his manager, you would know the root of the problem: His work-related role, values, and purpose are not synched. However, odds are that this peak performer is achieving both your goals for him and his personal, purpose-based goals for himself.

Employees who have clarified their personal values and vision and integrated them with their organization's stated values and vision are likely to be living, working, and even dancing purposefully.

Most organizations have a vision, mission, or purpose statement, but few employees have one for their work-related role. This is a lost opportunity and a shame. Without a noble purpose, what is enticing employees away from the daily bombardment of junk foods? Without a higher cause or sense of meaning, why give up those French fries or wait for the promised marshmallow?

Collaborate with your employees to find alignment between their perception of their role-related values and purpose and your perception. Come to conclusions together that meet both their needs and those of the organization. Acting with a noble purpose reflects the highest-quality self-regulation.

Motivation Mini Case Study: Self-Regulation and Mohammedan

Imagine three hundred pharmaceutical reps from the Middle East and Africa vying to win an iPad mini. The instructions were easy: Everyone stands up. I flip a coin. While the coin is in the air, everyone shouts out either heads or tails. If you guess wrong, you sit down. If you guess correctly, you stay standing for the next round. The rounds continue until only one person is left standing. That person wins the iPad mini.

The winner was Mohammedan from Egypt, who was so excited about winning the iPad mini that he bounded on stage to grab it, along with my microphone. It turns out Mohammedan was a pharmaceutical rep by day and a singer by night. He started singing in Arabic. All of a sudden, three hundred people were standing and singing with him—he sang a line; they responded with the same line. It was electric!

After the frivolity died down, I explained the Spectrum of Motivation model. We explored the horizontal axis of psychological needs and how all humans, regardless of culture, creed, race, gender, or generation, experience positive and sustainable energy, vitality, and a sense of well-being when their needs for autonomy, relatedness, and competence are satisfied. We explored the vertical axis of self-regulation. We did activities practicing how they could use the MVPs of mindfulness, values, and purpose to shift from a suboptimal motivational outlook to an optimal motivational outlook.

Things were going well until later that day the general manager of the region approached me: "Susan, we have a problem. Mohammedan cheated." "What do you mean, he cheated?" "He stayed standing even when he called out the wrong answer. He wants to return the iPad. What are we going to do?" The GM was distraught. But I saw a wonderful opportunity.

Mohammedan nervously agreed to share what he had learned and how he was feeling. He returned to the stage. He had written out his confession on paper. His hands were shaking as he read it aloud. He was full of emotion as he explained that now he understood he had been in the external motivational outlook during the heads-or-tails activity. He really wanted to win the iPad mini, but he also wanted to impress his colleagues and be the star of the moment. He also had become aware of his low-quality self-regulation—he had failed to live up to the organization's values, or his own, for honesty and integrity. He shared his surprise at how miserable he felt—despite winning the iPad mini. He realized it was because winning through cheating had not satisfied his psychological needs for autonomy, relatedness, and competence. He wanted to return the iPad so someone more deserving would have it.

Then something amazing happened. Mohammedan again had three hundred people standing and cheering—but this time for a very different reason. This time, people were moved to tears. I was one of them. Mohammedan was experiencing a higher-quality energy, vitality, and well-being that was generating a positive ripple effect among hundreds in that room. That moment was a glorious demonstration of motivation as a skill, which happens to be the focus of the following chapter.

Recapping "The Danger of Drive"

The danger of drive is that it promotes external motivators that undermine people's psychological needs for autonomy, relatedness, and competence—diminishing the quality and sustainability of their motivation. External motivational drivers come in tangible forms such as money, incentives, or a big office or title and intangible forms such as approval, status, shame, or fear. When employees focus on an external motivator, they are controlled by it, or whoever is doing the driving, and without realizing it, they lose autonomy.

People ultimately resent leaders who create a pressurized workplace that undermines autonomy. Moreover, people regard managers who drive for results as self-serving. They consider support by these managers as conditional: if you do as I say, then I will reward you in some way. Conditional support undermines people's relatedness.

Driving for results by adding pressure and tension blocks people's creativity and ability to focus, leaving them feeling inadequate or ineffective at coping with the circumstances—which undermines competence.

A direct connection exists between high-quality self-regulation and experiencing high-quality psychological needs. People can counteract everyday drivers that undermine their psychological needs for ARC by using high-quality self-regulation through the MVPs. This is the skill of motivation explored in chapter 4.

When employees thrive, leaders don't need to drive.

Motivation Is a Skill

Years ago, I met with Dr. Edward Deci, recognized as the father of and leading researcher in the field of intrinsic motivation. My purpose was to get his reaction to the model and framework my partners, David Facer and Drea Zigarmi, and I had developed to teach motivation as a skill. Revealing our Spectrum of Motivation model, I explained, "We imagine a whole new world at work where every individual accepts responsibility and takes the initiative to activate his or her own optimal motivation. Three skills are required for activating your own positive energy, vitality, and sense of well-being:

- *Identify your current motivational outlook* by recognizing and understanding your sense of well-being and your underlying reasons for doing what you are doing.

- *Shift to (or maintain) an optimal motivational outlook* by using the MVPs of self-regulation to satisfy your psychological needs for ARC.

- *Reflect* by noticing the difference between having a suboptimal motivational outlook and having an optimal motivational outlook."

After studying the model and three skills for a moment, Ed announced, "We are simpatico." Buoyed by his endorsement, I continued, "We also want to teach managers how to facilitate people using the three skills by having motivational outlook conversations!" Pause, long pause. Finally, Ed said, "Okay. But with a caveat. Leaders must understand how to do it for themselves before they can hope to guide others." He shook his head warily: "Can you imagine a manager who hates performance reviews conducting a review with the intention of motivating an employee? It will not end well."

We agreed. So with a clear mission, my partners and I set out to teach *leaders* how to apply the new science of motivation by *first* learning the three skills of motivation for *themselves*. But teaching leaders about their own motivation is much harder than we thought it would be! Not because leaders are closed to new ideas, not because they are satisfied with their current attempts to motivate people, and definitely not because they are okay with suboptimally motivated or disengaged employees. *Teaching leaders about motivation is difficult because they believe their job is to motivate others—not themselves.*

It could be that some leaders want control—or feel that they need it since they are being held accountable for motivated employees. Others might not feel like they're leading if they are not bossing, supervising, or managing someone.

Teaching leaders the three skills of motivation is also a challenge because they are so desperate for an instant or easy remedy to one of their greatest aggravations: disengaged employees. Leaders are responsible for achieving the goals of the organization *and* accountable for improving engagement scores. They want to know how to motivate people *now*. They have little patience for learning to use the skills of motivation for themselves and *then* facilitating others through a motivational shift.

Try This: Select a Challenging Task, Goal, or Situation

If you have low-quality motivation to learn the skills of motivation for yourself, try testing the three skills by applying them to an important task, goal, or situation. Make learning the three skills of motivation relevant to something significant in your professional or personal life.

As you read this chapter, personalize the content by choosing a task, goal, or situation where

- You are repeatedly procrastinating—such as submitting your expense reports late.

- Others are frustrated because you haven't handled it yet—such as approving a budget.

- You haven't had the courage to act—such as pursuing a great idea.

- Your energy drains just thinking about it—such as attending staff or committee meetings.

- Shifting your current outlook and seeing it from a fresh perspective would feel meaningful and worthwhile—such as resolving a conflict with a particularly difficult person.

When you focus on a specific goal, learning is more efficient. However, the three skills don't have to be goal focused. You can apply what you learn anytime you don't experience a positive sense of well-being in general, when your biorhythms just seem to be off, or when you find yourself in a bad mood.[1]

As you apply what you are learning to your personal example, I will use the example of dieting. Given the amount of money and extravagant incentives organizations dedicate to promoting health these days, weight loss and healthy eating have become relevant workplace goals. All of us have probably tackled diet and healthy eating goals at some point in our lives. Another interesting reason to use diet as the example is this: junk food and health food are more than handy metaphors for suboptimal and optimal motivational outlooks. Applying the skill of motivation may be the secret behind weaning yourself off *real* marshmallows and French fries—not just conceptual ones.

Activating Optimal Motivation

The three skills for activating optimal motivation are

1. Identify your current motivational outlook.

2. Shift to (or maintain) an optimal motivational outlook.

3. Reflect.

Skill 1: Identify your current motivational outlook

Select one of the six outlooks based on your intuitive understanding of each outlook. Refrain from judging whether your motivational outlook is good or bad—you are only identifying your current motivational outlook.

As I reflect on losing twenty-five pounds over the next six months, my motivational outlook options might be

- *Disinterested*—I see no value in losing twenty-five pounds. I may not be pleased with my weight or diet, but I have no intentions of acting on this goal—it is too overwhelming right now.

- *External*—I really want to win the prize our health insurance company is offering me if I achieve my weight-loss goal over the next six months.

- *Imposed*—I'm feeling a lot of pressure to lose the weight. My family members are worried about my health; I feel guilty about disappointing them.

- *Aligned*—I value my health, and losing weight is one way to be healthier. I look forward to losing twenty-five pounds. It is a healthy choice for me.

- *Integrated*—Part of my life purpose is to be a role model for my children and to have the energy I need to be involved in their lives. Losing twenty-five pounds is a way of gaining the energy and vitality I need to fulfill my purpose.

- *Inherent*—I am enthusiastic about losing the weight. This new diet sounds fun and exciting. I enjoy trying new things.

Now look *behind* the motivational outlook you identified for confirmation. Referring to the Spectrum of Motivation model at the front of the book, answer these questions:

- Would you describe your satisfaction of psychological needs (ARC) as high quality or low quality?

- Is the quality of your self-regulation (use of MVPs) related to your goal high or low?

- Are your needs for ARC being satisfied or not?

- Are you employing the MVPs to self-regulate?

For the weight-loss goal, I might answer with these insights into my psychological needs:

- As soon as I told myself I was going on a diet and couldn't eat anything I really liked, my autonomy was eroded. Now I have the urge to eat everything I told myself not to eat! I find myself compensating for my low-quality autonomy by eating all the stuff I'm not supposed to eat. Then I feel guilty and mad at myself.

- I am going on this diet to appease my doctor and family. I am afraid of disappointing them. Sometimes I find myself resenting their interference. My fear of not living up to their expectations, potential shame, and guilt from eating what I'm not supposed to eat leave me with low-quality relatedness with my doctor, my family, and myself!

- My competence is shot. The pressure from my doctor and family members makes it clear they don't trust my ability to take care of myself. Maybe they are right; maybe I have failed to do what is right for me. I am not confident I will be successful on this diet. When I've lost weight in the past, I always seemed to gain it—and more—back again.

These statements may sound familiar to anyone who has tried to lose weight. They are examples of low-quality psychological needs. It's no wonder so many of us give up on diets!

Now consider the quality of your self-regulation. How would you rate the MVPs? For the weight-loss goal, for example, I might make these statements about the quality of my mindfulness, values, and purpose:

- I have not practiced mindfulness. When I eat food I am not supposed to eat, I try not to think about it. I tell myself that I'll start the diet for real next week after I finish the report that is due on Friday.

- I never thought about aligning my values to my eating habits. I haven't considered why this goal is meaningful or important—other than skinny is better than fat, I guess. I apply my values for integrity, loyalty, and honesty to the reports I create at work, but I don't understand how they relate to what I eat.

- I have not connected to a life- or work-related purpose statement because I don't have one. Who has time to write a purpose statement? I'm too busy living my life and supporting a family!

In each of the statements, I described low-quality ARC and MVPs—implying a *suboptimal* motivational outlook. I have identified an imposed motivational outlook expressed through feelings of manipulation, resentment, fear, and shame.

After exploring the quality of your psychological needs and self-regulation, what conclusions did you reach for your own task, goal, or situation? What is your current motivational outlook? Does it match the motivational outlook you identified intuitively at the beginning of this section? Are you ready for skill 2?

Skill 2: Shift to (or maintain) an optimal motivational outlook

In the first skill, you identified your current motivational outlook, so you know where you are. Skill 2 involves choosing where you want to be—which motivational outlook is preferable—and implementing a strategy for getting there. To make a good choice, consider the distinctions among the six motivational outlooks.

Each outlook carries with it pros, cons, opportunities, challenges, and major implications for how, or if, you achieve your goals and sustain your success.

Shifting to the disinterested motivational outlook. The good news about having the disinterested motivational outlook is that you can avoid spending energy you don't have and you don't have to change anything. The bad news is that you don't have any energy and nothing will change.

If you are going through the motions without any real need to get or stay involved with your goal, you are in the disinterested motivational outlook with statements in your head such as *I am not interested. It does not matter to me. I am not concerned about who wants me to do the work. I do not have the energy for managing this goal or situation.*

If you were in the disinterested motivational outlook for your learning goal, you might be reading a thrilling novel right now instead of this book. For the weight-loss goal, I would be in a disinterested motivational outlook if I gave lip service to a diet by sitting here eating an order of French fries.

The critical question is, Given the choice, why would you ever want to be, or stay, in the disinterested motivational outlook? You have a spectrum of motivational possibilities. Why choose to be where there is nothing to gain and opportunities to lose?

Shifting to the external motivational outlook. Promises, promises. The external motivational outlook is all about doing something in return for a promise of a tangible or intangible reward. A tangible reward is what one character requests in the famous line from the movie *Jerry Maguire:* "Show me the money!" You can replace *the money* in that line with *a bonus, a raise, an incentive, a reward, the corner office, first place, an impressive title,* or *a trophy.* Intangible rewards include attention, political clout, power, status, acceptance, public recognition, private praise, or other people's admiration.

Unfortunately, promising external rewards is the go-to motivation strategy promoted in most organizations because even though they may be expensive, they don't require much effort or creativity beyond coming up with the next big contest, repackaging reward programs, or acquiring funding. You may find those in the hierarchy reinforcing this motivational outlook since it was their idea and it promotes outcomes they want.

In the external motivational outlook, you hear yourself saying statements such as *I am choosing to get involved because it affords me a certain lifestyle. If I do this work now, it could really look good on my resume. I will win the respect and recognition of my coworkers. I will do it, but I will need a monetary reward, public recognition, or a promotion for it.*

This is an enticing motivational outlook—those external rewards can be hard to resist. You would be wise to remember that the external motivational outlook is the junk food of motivation that undermines your psychological needs for ARC. You might experience an initial rush of energy that catapults you into action as you dream of the rewards promised in return for your efforts. But beware; your creativity, innovation, and patience for achieving excellence may suffer because your eye is on the prize instead of the goal itself. Along the way, you might earn prestige and recognition for your efforts. But you may find that your fame is fleeting. You could benefit from the skill you acquire as you pursue your goal. But your skill could be undermined as you take shortcuts in pursuit of winning.

Still, you rationalize that the external motivational outlook is a good one. Winning is proof that you are worth something. Power means you have the clout to get things done. Why would you want to shift from this outlook?

The hidden costs and opportunity losses of banking on the external motivational outlook are rarely worth the potential short-term gains.

In my weight-loss example, if I were to achieve my weight-loss goal to win the prize offered by our health-care company, to impress people, or in hopes of earning someone's love, any success would likely be short lived and much less satisfying than I imagined.[2]

If you are currently in the external motivational outlook, the potential *loss* of creativity, innovation, quality, productivity, and mental and physical health, as well as the ultimate lack of ARC, makes it worth considering a shift to a more optimal motivational outlook.

Shifting to the imposed motivational outlook. The imposed motivational outlook is one of the unhealthiest of the junk-food outlooks! We tend to spend a lot of time in this outlook—doing tasks or pursuing goals because we think we *have* to or to avoid negative emotions of guilt, shame, and fear.

In the imposed motivational outlook, you hear yourself saying statements such as *I have to do it. I am obligated to participate. I'll feel guilty if I don't do it. I would be ashamed of not doing it. There is a lot of pressure to get this done and I am afraid I might not be able to do it. I need to prove myself. I am afraid of disappointing others. I am afraid of disappointing myself!*

Sometimes you can almost justify your imposed motivational outlook if you think that caving into pressures to "do it their way" is more likely to help you keep your job. You can even rationalize that the reason you are fearful of disappointing someone is that you care about the person. However, relatedness is about mutually caring relationships without ulterior motives; it is pure and free of pressure, stress, or obligation to prove you care. For example, losing weight from fear of disappointing your spouse is different from losing weight as an act of loving your spouse. This is a subtle but critical distinction.

Relatedness is not about appeasing someone, keeping the peace with her, or worrying that she might retreat from the relationship if you don't live up to her expectations.

Who or what, would you guess, plays the biggest role in putting you in the imposed motivational outlook? Have you ever accepted a meeting invitation and then, when the meeting time rolled around, thought, *I don't want to go to that meeting!* You accepted the invitation; you have to go. You would feel guilty if you did not show up. You fear losing the respect of people who matter. You are feeling manipulated and pressured. You might start feeling resentful. These thoughts and emotions undermine your autonomy—the perception that you have a choice. You were the one who accepted the meeting invitation—along with pressure to go and the guilt, shame, and fear of not going.

The irony of the imposed motivational outlook is that the one who does the most imposing is probably you.

In my weight-loss example, the pressure, resentment, and fear of failure that described my experience also describes the imposed motivational outlook. If you are in the imposed motivational outlook for your own task, goal, or situation, seriously consider choosing one of the next three optimal outlooks instead.

Shifting to the aligned motivational outlook. In the aligned motivational outlook you go beyond achieving your goal to making meaning. You are in the aligned motivational outlook when what you're doing is linked to your values. You experience a positive sense of well-being from the satisfaction of aligning goals to values. When you can link your own values to someone else's request of you, you are more likely to find meaning as you take action.

In the aligned motivational outlook, you hear yourself saying statements such as *I volunteered for this; I am not being coerced into it. I have thought it through, and participating and working hard at it are important to me. I might not have chosen it for myself, but I still agree with it and own it. I agree with your rationale on why this is important.*

For all its positives, the aligned motivational outlook has a couple of challenges to consider. For one, to align with values, you need to have developed values. For another, your current actions could appear selfish to others if you have not declared your values and clarified your intentions. Still, the pros outweigh the cons.

Shifting from a suboptimal motivational outlook to the aligned motivational outlook has bountiful benefits. Acting from your developed values reflects high-quality self-regulation and results in high-quality psychological needs. You satisfy your need for autonomy as you make choices based on your values—you feel in control of your actions. You satisfy your need for relatedness as your goal is in harmony with important values and your actions create a sense of meaning. You satisfy your need for competence as you focus your energy creatively and productively.

In my weight-loss example, I would experience a genuine improvement in my energy, vitality, and sense of well-being with a shift from the imposed motivational outlook to the aligned motivational outlook.

In your own example, the shift from a suboptimal to an aligned motivational outlook would be a vast improvement. But you have other choices to consider as well—the integrated and inherent motivational outlooks.

Shifting to the integrated motivational outlook. When you are in the integrated motivational outlook, your developed values are less conscious and more second nature. You identify with what is asked or required of you. When you take action, you share your best self. You feel a level of commitment. Your emotional state is deeply positive. You are acting with a noble purpose.

In the integrated motivational outlook, you hear yourself saying statements such as *Working on this is extremely meaningful to me. I want to stay engaged in this because it taps into my sense of purpose. I understand what is being asked of me and it is integrated with who I am. It lets me be authentic. Working on this is part of how I have decided to live my life. I notice that obstacles do not derail me. I am committed to doing the work and moving forward.* Money and rewards are by-products of doing purpose-filled work.

If you detect that the integrated motivational outlook is mostly positive, you would be right. Your energy, vitality, and sense of well-being are the highest quality when you act from an authentic, peaceful, and purposeful place. The only downside? You need to have a sense of purpose!

In my weight-loss example, being able to shift from the imposed motivational outlook to an integrated motivational outlook would generate an entirely different quality of energy and probability of both short-term and long-term success.

In your personal example, if you are able to fulfill a deeper purpose through your task, goal, or situation, chances are that you are in the integrated motivational outlook. Consider how your goal might fulfill a noble purpose. Shifting to the integrated motivational outlook is always worth the effort when you do not feel an inner calm along with the positive energy.

When you are in the integrated motivational outlook, you feel a sense of peace. This is the outlook where your longings are most deeply satisfied.

Shifting to the inherent motivational outlook. In the inherent motivational outlook, you have a natural, often-unexplainable interest in and enjoyment for what you are doing. Your task, goal, or situation might require a lot of your energy, but it is a good kind of energy. You often lose track of time because you are enjoying yourself so much.

In the inherent motivational outlook, you hear yourself saying statements such as *I don't know why I do it. I don't think about it—I just like it. It's fun. I find it interesting. It is easy to get lost in this work—that is how much pleasure I get from it. I do not think in terms of needing tangible or intangible rewards. Doing the activity itself is reward enough. Even though I know this is part of my job and money is involved, I don't do it for that reason. Doing this work is about digging in and having fun. I enjoy this work and get satisfaction from accomplishing difficult challenges related to it.*

To determine activities where you are most likely to either be in or get into the inherent motivational outlook, think about what you do when you have time on your hands. Adults have too few moments that are not filled with "busyness," so you may need to reflect back on when you were a child and had more time for discretionary activities.

It was enlightening to think back and remember what I loved to do when I was eight years old. I spent hours designing and crafting workbooks out of Big Chief writing tablets to teach my siblings how to read before they ever entered school. Today, one of my greatest joys comes from designing workshops, teaching, and writing.

The inherent motivational outlook is the most naturally intrinsic outlook—what you are doing is a reward in and of itself and you don't require external prompts or incentives.

Getting in the flow. Have you ever been so immersed in an activity that you were shocked when you finally noticed how much time had passed? Time flew by without your conscious awareness.

When in a state of flow, you are energized, focused, and fully absorbed by what you are doing. You are also more productive, creative, and emotionally healthy.[3]

You are most likely to get in the flow in either the integrated or the inherent motivational outlook. Flow can occur when you are in the aligned motivational outlook; however, it is more likely to occur when what you are doing is second nature and less dependent on consciously chosen values and goals.

Flow is very good when you are in the integrated motivational outlook with a sense of meaning and purpose. Flow

could also be good in the inherent motivational outlook—or
not. It depends on the activity.

**A potential downside of flow in the inherent motivational
outlook.** Have you ever been lured into playing a video
game or app? It encourages your learning, provides you
choices, and matches your competence with the challenge
at hand. It is food for flow. Time flies.

When you finally move away from the game, how do
you feel? If you feel relaxed and refreshed and ready to
take on more meaningful goals and activities, that's great!
Your game playing provided a respite and paid positive
dividends.

But have you ever felt a little guilty with the amount of
time you spend on games? Consider why. Sometimes it is
easier to enjoy yourself than acting on developed values or
fulfilling a noble purpose. You may have enjoyed playing
the games, but at what cost?

If you love an activity for the sake of the activity itself,
you have an inherent motivational outlook—and that can
be wonderful. If you love an activity *and* are able to link it
to developed values and a noble purpose, you have an integrated motivational outlook—and that is *definitely a good
thing*. The Spectrum of Motivation provides you choices for
satisfying your psychological needs and experiencing positive energy, vitality, and a sense of well-being.

**The inherent motivational outlook dips on the Spectrum
of Motivation model.** You may have noticed the curve on
the model. The inherent motivational outlook takes a dip
because it doesn't take high-quality self-regulation to do

what is really fun and natural to do. Just because something is fun does not mean it is fulfilling all three psychological needs—especially relatedness. (Millions of youngsters are in the inherent motivational outlook, spending hours playing electronic games while putting their physical health at risk, not to mention their social skills.)

Acting on your values and purpose requires higher-quality self-regulation. It turns out that putting that game away and consciously using your time and talent for more values-based activities generates more physical, mental, and social well-being.

Remember, the Spectrum of Motivation is not a continuum—you can be at any motivational outlook at any time and shift to any other outlook in a moment.

Optimal choices: shifting to the aligned, integrated, and inherent motivational outlooks. You will see real benefits in terms of positive energy, health, creativity, short-term achievements, and long-term gains when you are in or shift to one of the three optimal motivational outlooks. But realistically, fewer opportunities exist at work for experiencing the pure fun and intrinsic satisfaction that come from the inherent motivational outlook. This is why having two other optimal choices—the aligned and integrated motivational outlooks—which are based on values, purpose, and meaning, is so important to the quality of motivation at work.

Making the shift. The aim of shifting is to satisfy your psychological needs for ARC. The means for shifting is self-regulation. Here are suggestions for using high-quality self-regulation through the MVPs—mindfulness, values, and purpose.

- *Practice mindfulness*—Here are two ways to practice mindfulness:

  - Take a mindfulness moment—By the time you have mindfully chosen which motivational outlook you want to shift to, you may have already shifted! The process of identifying your current motivational outlook and considering if there is a preferable option is a form of mindfulness that can generate an automatic shift.

    But often, a shift requires deliberation and a conscious choice. This is when you need to take a mindfulness moment. Donna, a plant manager in Florida, tells how she decided to be more mindful by simply taking a few minutes before meetings and phone calls to explore how she was feeling, practice being nonjudgmental, and be open to what might happen next. She also admitted that because of her natural personality, intensified by being a woman in a man's world, she had a reputation for being fiery, outspoken, and quick to respond. Donna reported, "I felt calmer, but it didn't seem like such a big deal until two weeks after I started my mindfulness moments. My teenage daughter, who never seemed to notice or comment on anything I did unless it embarrassed her, said to me one evening, 'Mom, what's going on? You seem so different—you're not stressed out.' I was stunned. If my daughter noticed, it was a big deal."

- Use the "Power of Why"—If you have been assigned a task you are disinterested in doing, are doing only for the money, or feel obligated to do, ask yourself why you don't want to do it. Then with each answer, follow up with another why question. Asking why, why, why helps you peel through the layers of distractions, and eventually you will figure out that you have a choice (autonomy), can find some meaning or purpose (relatedness), and will learn and grow from the experience (competence). Asking why provides a mindfulness method for getting connected to psychological needs that were being obscured through your suboptimal interpretation of the assignment.

- *Align with developed values*—Ask yourself what you value more than what you are getting from your current suboptimal outlook. If you are about to eat a bunch of French fries, ask yourself what you value more than French fries—such as your health and well-being. If you are about to send a nasty e-mail because someone made a decision you disagree with, ask yourself what you value more—proving you are right or collaborating for a better outcome? If you are about to work overtime again, ask what you value more than the money or power you are working for—such as having dinner with your family or tucking your kids into bed.

- *Connect with a noble purpose*—In the introduction to this book, I wrote that I finally understood how I was able to change from a meat-loving omnivore to a strict vegetarian overnight—and sustain the decision. Almost thirty years ago, I was watching a segment of a news-based television show called *20/20* on how we treat the animals we eat when I felt a distinct shift in my perspective. I realized in that moment that I would never eat meat again. I did not base my decision on feelings of guilt or shame; I was not acting out of my own health concerns. In that moment I recognized a profound sense of wanting to do my part to make the world less violent and more peaceful, less habitual and more conscious, and less self-serving and more attuned to the welfare of the whole. What others describe as being disciplined, I have come to understand as acting from a deep conviction that comes from a noble purpose. Few events in life are more powerful than making important decisions from a sense of purpose.

The next chapter provides examples of how you can use these strategies with the people you lead. But of course, it is always best to practice them on yourself first!

Shifting all over the place. Over a decade ago, I held a short training session for a small group of volunteers willing to let me try out my ideas for applying the new science of motivation. After I explained the six motivational outlooks, a young man named Mark asked for clarity. "My wife loves Valentine's Day and wants to celebrate it with a romantic dinner, a gift, flowers, chocolates—the whole thing. I hate it. I feel it is a holiday created by retailers to sell more stuff. I resent being told that I should love my wife in a certain way on February 14. I love my wife all year long. What's so special about this one day? Is this a good example of the imposed motivational outlook?"

Mark had a lot of heads (mostly men's) nodding in the room. I asked him how he handled the situation. He said, "Oh, I go along with it." I asked him why. He replied, "Because I am afraid of what might happen the rest of the year if I didn't." We laughed, but it was a telling comment. Mark was motivated to celebrate Valentine's Day, but remember, a person is always motivated. The real issue was *why* he was motivated. It was obvious that the issue was negatively affecting his energy. Mark was celebrating Valentine's Day in the imposed motivational outlook. I don't know for sure, but I bet his wife could sense it.

I asked him one question: "Do you love your wife enough to love her the way she wants to be loved on February 14?" Mark didn't need to love Valentine's Day. He needed to get in touch with the love he had for his wife. Then he could link his love for his wife to the task of celebrating the day. Mark "got it" and said he would do just that.

Jump forward ten years. I found myself at a conference, sitting next to Mark at breakfast. "Oh, Mark! I am speaking on motivation later this morning and planned to tell your Valentine's Day story. I have used it for years as a great example of the imposed motivational outlook but never with you in the room. Are you comfortable with me sharing it today?" Mark looked at me dumbfounded. "I have no idea what you are talking about, Susan."

I reminded him of that little session ten years ago, about his resentment of Valentine's Day and his commitment to love his wife enough to go through with the celebration. He had no recollection of the incident at all. I was devastated. Integrity is one of my core values and I refuse to tell made-up stories in my work. Mark understood my regret and assured me that he had a poor memory. Since it was a good story, he gave me permission to tell the story. I was hesitant but decided to take him up on the offer.

A couple of hours later, I was telling Mark's story. I acknowledged to the group that Mark was in the room. I got to the part where he made the shift to focus on his love of his wife rather than his dislike of Valentine's Day, when all of a sudden Mark yelled out loud, "Susan! I remember!"

The whole room turned toward Mark. He explained what had transpired at breakfast and said that he had given me permission to use the story even though he couldn't recall the event. Then he said, "I remember now that Susan guided me to a different mind-set about Valentine's Day. I made it a big deal—and it was actually fun. In fact, my wife and I enjoyed it so much that we decided to make it a yearly ritual. Over the years, we have expanded it to a Valentine's weekend—we get the grandparents to take care of the kids, and my wife and I go away to a romantic place and have a wonderful weekend together. It's become such a part of who we are as a couple that I forgot I ever hated Valentine's Day! Susan, does that mean that now I am in the integrated motivational outlook?"

It was one of those remarkable moments for a speaker—when what you had planned falls apart and something better than you could imagine takes its place. Of course, Mark was right. His initial efforts for celebrating Valentine's Day were conscious and conscientious, based on developed values. Clearly, in the beginning he shifted from the imposed to the aligned motivational outlook. Years of practice now had him, with his wife, celebrating Valentine's weekend in the integrated motivational outlook.

When it comes to celebrating that special Valentine's Weekend, Mark's wife was in the inherent motivational outlook—she always loved celebrating Valentine's Day. Mark may now share her passion and enjoyment, but he is in the integrated motivational outlook—he never had a pure intrinsic love of the holiday. As he acted on his values over time, the celebration became an integrated part of his life.

Shifting to the integrated motivational outlook comes through choices you make based on values or a sense of purpose that have become second nature, self-identifying activities, or part of your reason for being.

Skill 3: Reflect

To reflect, begin by asking yourself how you feel after your shifting experience. Your feelings are the pathway to understanding your well-being. And recognizing your well-being is at the heart of maintaining an optimal motivational outlook.

Reflecting may prove to be a difficult challenge if you are a leader who believes there is no room for feelings in the workplace.

Here is the point: you have feelings whether you like it or not. Through the appraisal process described in chapter 1, you reach conclusions about your place in the world through both cognitive and affective means—through thoughts and emotions. Research indicates that feelings reflected through emotions are by far the greatest influencers of whether you experience a positive sense of well-being or not. And remember, well-being leads to positive intentions and, ultimately, positive behavior.[4]

Well-being is at the heart of your motivational outlook. You might like to know what you are looking for as you examine your sense of well-being. Positive well-being has the specific characteristics listed below. A lack of well-being is just the opposite of these characteristics.[5]

- The presence of positive energy
- A sense of physical and emotional harmony
- Calm from being in supportive and secure relationships
- Little to no negative energy, stress, or anxiety
- A sense of continued learning, personal growth, and accomplishment
- A feeling that one's work is contributing to something socially meaningful

Before you slight well-being as too "fluffy," consider the perspective of Dr. Dirk Veldhort, director of corporate health for global manufacturer AkzoNobel, headquartered in Amsterdam. When I asked what keeps him awake at night, he responded, "The health and well-being of fifty-five thousand people around the world." When I asked why this is so important, Dirk was adamant: "Well-being is a means to an end. With it, you can create value for yourself and your organization. Without it, short-term productivity is less probable and long-term growth is almost impossible."

Dirk has overseen the doctoring of hundreds, if not thousands, of employees—many high-ranking executives—back to health after they have crashed from working too many hours or eating too much junk food while chasing external goals. But he reminds us, "Even passionate leaders often push themselves so far that they do a disservice to themselves and ultimately those they lead by not paying attention to their own well-being. I applaud the work you are doing in this field. Well-being is not fluffy—it is essential to our personal and professional quality of life and sustained performance."

How do you pay attention to your well-being? Your greatest insight will come through understanding your emotions and moods. Many leaders are out of touch with their emotions and try to ignore their moods, especially at work. Ironically, the more you overlook your emotions, the more those emotions tend to rule your behavior. Your blindness to emotions limits you to dysfunctional patterns of behavior, ill equipping you to adapt to the needs of the moment.

If you are going to become adept at managing your appraisal process—and helping others manage theirs—you must be adept at reflecting: acknowledging, recognizing, identifying, and accepting your feelings.[6]

When you consider your goal, do you have a sense of positives well-being? If my goal example is to lose twenty-five pounds over the next six months, I need to reflect by asking myself, How do I feel about it? What physical sensations do I get when I reflect on my goal example of losing twenty-five pounds? Just thinking about it might make my eye twitch, my stomach tighten, or my jaw clench. I might get sleepy or lethargic. Recognizing my physical sensations, I then realize my opinion, judgment, or interpretation of the physical sensations—emotions such as fear, regret, discouragement, resentfulness, or sadness. These unpleasant emotions will erode any sense of positive well-being.

Of course, when I think about losing twenty-five pounds over the next six months I could also experience butterflies in my stomach, a warm glow, or a burst of energy that signal anticipation, calm, and eagerness. I could interpret those physical sensations as pleasant emotions such as excitement, openness, and confidence. I could conclude through this appraisal process that I am experiencing a *positive* sense of well-being.

This is an interesting phenomenon worth noting. You can experience both positive well-being and a lack of it for the same goal. For example, I might feel a positive sense of well-being when I think about how losing weight will give me newfound energy but get depressed when I think about how long it is going to take. The beauty of understanding your well-being is that if you have not yet shifted to an optimal motivational outlook, you can use the power of the positive to overcome the nagging negative.

If you used the first two skills to shift successfully, the third skill will help you maintain your optimal motivational outlook. If you still have a suboptimal motivational outlook, using the third skill to reflect on your situation provides another opportunity to shift. Either way, ask yourself how you feel about the goal example you selected. Do you have a positive sense of well-being or not?

One European client shared, "Optimal motivation was like a time bomb for me. I was at my desk dreading a meeting that was starting in ten minutes. As I reflected on how

I was feeling, the training you conducted came to light. I realized I had an imposed motivational outlook. I could choose to stay there, be miserable, complain, and waste my time in the meeting, or I could shift. I chose to shift. It was my aha motivation moment."

Your shift to an optimal motivational outlook will happen in a flash or evolve as you go about living your life. Either way, your shift is a result of reflecting on the present moment and realizing you have options.

Reflecting on your suboptimal motivational outlook can make shifting to an optimal motivational outlook more compelling. Observe how debilitating your lack of energy is in the disinterested motivational outlook. Notice how your energy stimulated by the initial thrill of the external motivational outlook wanes when the stimulus is gone. Notice how your energy prompted by the guilt, shame, obligation, disappointment, resentment, or anger of the imposed motivational outlook demands more energy to keep fueling these negative emotions.

On the other hand, if you shifted to an optimal motivational outlook, reflecting helps you appreciate the quality of energy generated through meaningful values in the aligned motivational outlook. Reflection promotes awareness of the high-quality energy emanating from the integrated motivational outlook when a noble, deeply felt purpose is realized. Reflecting reminds you to be grateful for the positive and sustainable energy of the inherent motivational outlook when you are doing what you naturally enjoy doing. Reflecting heightens your experience of ARC.

Good things happen when you shift to or maintain an optimal motivational outlook. Take the time to reflect on those good things. They are what keep you coming back for more.

Motivation Mini Case Study: Leader, Heal Thyself

Elaine Brink is senior vice president of zone sales for Express Employment Professionals. When she attended the Optimal Motivation training, her intention was to learn how to motivate her staff and franchise owners in one of the country's most successful staffing agencies. Even though she learned that motivating people doesn't work, she still got more than she bargained for.

"We were asked to learn how to activate optimal motivation for ourselves before applying it with others," explained Elaine. "At first, it was difficult for me because I thought, 'I don't need this; I'm good.'" As part of the training, Elaine decided to work on an assignment planning and producing an important event outside the United States.

Skill 1: Identify your current motivational outlook

As she worked through the first skill, Elaine realized her sense of well-being was undermined just thinking about the event. She described herself as a no-nonsense, high-energy, get-it-done type of person: "I was getting the job done and gritting my teeth through the entire experience."

It became obvious to Elaine that she was working from an imposed motivational outlook—resentful that she was stuck with a highly unreasonable timeline with no input on the dates. That's when a flood of emotion hit her. She suddenly got in touch with how her negative attitude was infecting her entire team—not only the people she needed to do the job well but also the people she cared about. "Everything I touched was tainted by my suboptimal motivational outlook."

Skill 2: Shift to (or maintain) an optimal motivational outlook

When Elaine got to skill 2 she was able to shift from an imposed to an aligned motivational outlook by aligning her goal to her developed values. "I had not taken the time to consider how important the event was to our business, how appreciative I was to be trusted enough to be put in charge, or how grateful I was to have the skills and experience to pull it off. For the first time, I saw this as an opportunity to develop members of my staff. I was in a position to help them gain skills and experience that would serve them and the organization moving forward. It also dawned on me that I was the one who accepted the offer to take on the event—I could have said no, but I didn't."

Skill 3: Reflect

Elaine said, "I felt an immediate shift in my energy level. I knew I could sustain this positive sense of well-being, even during challenging times, because of the depth of my emotional connection to my values."

Elaine has continued to reflect on her shifting experience: "I now have a template for understanding my well-being, intentions, and leadership behaviors—and either shifting to or maintaining an optimal motivational outlook. I have also become much more consciously aware that I might be imposing goals and deadlines on other people. I wondered why leaders do this. My great aha is that sometimes as leaders we delegate goals and deadlines to others based on our own enthusiasm, values, and purpose without taking the time to understand how what we are delegating lands for the people who must carry our ideas through to completion."

Recapping "Motivation Is a Skill"

The three skills of motivation appear simple: Identify your current motivational outlook, shift to or maintain an optimal motivational outlook, and reflect on your energy, vitality, and sense of well-being. The skills may be simple, but the results are profound.

Thousands of studies dedicated to understanding human motivation and flourishing point to astounding benefits, such as greater mental and physical health, when people experience optimal motivational. More specifically, people who work with an optimal motivational outlook generate significant business outcomes when compared to employees working with suboptimal motivational outlooks.[7] They

- Deliver higher productivity

- Demonstrate higher creativity

- Generate increased sales

- Are more engaged and satisfied by their jobs

- Are more likely to be considered for or receive a promotion

You will experience these benefits whether applying the three skills of motivation to your own situation or facilitating someone else's shift, which happens to be the topic of chapter 5.

5.

Making Shift Happen

A colleague of mine manages a high-tech team. She was lamenting an experience trying to motivate a team member who often works from home. The team was growing, office space was tight, and one of the only offices with four walls and a door belonged to this team member. The manager asked the team member if he would give up his rarely used office to another team member who would benefit from the added space and privacy. The second team member's role required her to come in every day, and working in a cubicle was not conducive to her productivity.

The manager didn't want to "demotivate" the first team member by demanding he give up his office, but she thought it was a reasonable request, given that he usually worked from home. His response was an unexpected and flat-out rejection. Interestingly, in his refusal to give up his office, he admitted he didn't feel good about himself and wasn't proud of his decision, but he justified his stand by explaining that he had earned that space and it was important to his identity, rank, and position within the team.

The manager was disappointed by the outcome and blamed herself. She had recently heard that people are motivated by "status," and she had made the mistake of trying to remove his symbol of status.[1] She gave up on the idea, and the other team member continued to labor in less than optimal conditions.

This was a missed opportunity. The manager couldn't have motivated the first team member, but she could have facilitated a motivational outlook conversation to help him understand his own feelings and values regarding the situation.

A motivational outlook conversation is an informal or formal opportunity to facilitate a person's shift to an optimal motivational outlook. For brevity's sake, I'll refer to these as "outlook conversations."

When Should You Conduct an Outlook Conversation?

I cannot guarantee that the manager would have succeeded in changing the outcome of the office issue by having an outlook conversation, but I can guarantee that the team member would have had a greater chance to explore his values and take a stand that felt better to him—and probably to the entire team.

Ultimately, a shift depends on how an individual internalizes the situation and the options. Motivating people doesn't work because you cannot control someone else's internalization process.[2] If you try, the likely result is an imposed motivational outlook. Outlook conversations don't guarantee a shift to an optimal motivational outlook, but at the very least, they provide an opportunity for growth and understanding.

With no real control or guarantees that a person will shift from a suboptimal to an optimal motivational outlook (or sustain an optimal one), you might wonder, *Why bother?* It is a good and valid question.

An outlook conversation may be appropriate when a situation is negatively affecting the individual—or the person's outlook is negatively affecting the team or the organization. For example, outlook conversations are probably worth the effort when a person

- Misses deadlines, resulting in negative consequences for others

- Is performing below standard expectations on important goals or projects

- Doesn't seem to be living up to his potential in his role

- Is often in a bad mood that permeates the workplace

- Doesn't take initiative in circumstances where it is needed

- Displays emotion that is out of character or seems disproportionate to the situation

- Is undermining the positive energy of others

- Rejects helpful feedback

- Gets defensive easily or often

- Has values that seem out of alignment with the organization's purpose and values

- Is ignoring health and safety issues (his own or others')

You may need to have an outlook conversation with an individual for your own reasons—or for your own sake. For example, an outlook conversation may be appropriate when you

- Think an individual needs help or you want to offer your support

- See untapped potential and want to promote the individual's growth

- Stay awake at night thinking about the situation

- Are frustrated because nothing you say or do to make the situation better seems to matter

- Get angry when you think about the situation

- Are afraid or hesitant to deal with the situation

- Experience tension, stress, or impatience related to the situation

- Experience an energy drain just thinking about it

When I think about the angst my colleague had around the office issue, I believe an outlook conversation would have been good to have. However, as a leader, you need to determine if you are willing and able to dedicate the time and emotional labor to conduct an outlook conversation. Is it worth the effort for both you and the person you are facilitating?

Outlook Conversations—What Doesn't Work

Less-than-successful outlook conversations I have conducted were the result of three specific "do not do this" reasons. I hope you might appreciate learning what to avoid from my awkward experiences. Thankfully, no permanent damage was inflicted to the already suboptimally motivated individuals. But these were definitely opportunities missed. To conduct a satisfying outlook conversation—for both you and most importantly, the beneficiary of the conversation— avoid the three common mistakes:

- Do *not* problem solve.
- Do *not* impose your values.
- Do *not* expect a shift.

Do *not* problem solve

Bite your tongue. Take off your "I've been where you are and know how to solve your problem" hat. You will be sorely tempted to share your expertise, but do not confuse an outlook conversation with a problem-solving session.

When people have a suboptimal motivational outlook, it is almost impossible for them to engage in problem solving, let alone follow through on potential solutions. Facilitate a person's shift to an optimal motivational outlook before proceeding to problem solving and action planning.

Do *not* impose your values

Don't let your good intentions get in the way of your outcomes. One of the biggest mistakes leaders make is assuming another person holds or appreciates the same values.

Despite your good intentions, imposing your values on others tends to provoke an imposed motivational outlook.

Do *not* expect a shift

Refrain from "leading the witness." Relax, practice mindfulness, and allow the conversation to take its course. The outlook conversation is not about you or your ego. Realize that a person may not shift during your conversation. The shift may be a "time bomb" that goes off when the person is ready.

You will gain understanding, but remember, the purpose of an outlook conversation is to guide individuals to their own understanding of their motivational options and then shift, if they choose to do so.

Outlook Conversations—What *Does* Work

Practice patience. Follow the process. And be sensitive to what's happening in the moment. You are less likely to jump into problem solving, impose your values, or lead with expectations when you do three things:

- Prepare.

- Trust the process.

- Reflect and close.

Prepare

When I ask leaders what it takes to prepare for an outlook conversation, they typically respond with tried-and-true actions: clarify the topic, do your homework, check your facts, identify specific behaviors or examples as evidence, and so on. However, they almost always leave out the most critical aspect of preparation—shifting their own motivational outlook.

Preparing yourself may be the most important action for the success of your outlook conversation. Before entering any outlook conversation, check your own motivational outlook.

Preparing for outlook conversations is an ongoing effort. You need to be conscious and conscientious about the values you demonstrate as a leader. This doesn't mean you become inflexible, dogmatic, or unreasonable when faced with alternative values during an outlook conversation. It does mean that you have a position where you can compare and contrast alternative ideas in the best interest of the person and the situation you are facilitating.

You probably know that your values influence your approach to leadership. What may be a revelation, however, is how much your values—and especially your people's *perceptions* of your values—influence their quality of motivation. Research shows that the commitment people have to their leader and the organization is profoundly shaped by their perceptions of what the leader values.[3]

To prepare, examine your own sense of well-being regarding the upcoming conversation. Identify your current motivational outlook and choose a more appropriate or desired motivational outlook if necessary. Then shift your motivational outlook by linking your developed values to the upcoming outlook conversation—or consider how you will sustain the optimal outlook you have. If you have not shifted your own motivational outlook, how can you facilitate someone else's shift?

Your shift to an optimal motivational outlook in preparation for conducting an outlook conversation enables you to give those you lead a generous gift—your mindful, non-judgmental attention.

Trust the process

Follow the three skills for activating optimal motivation as guidelines. Remember this caveat—if you cannot practice the skills of activating optimal motivation for yourself, it is unlikely you will succeed in activating them with others.

- *Facilitate skill 1: Identify the person's current motivational outlook*—Get permission to explore the individual's feelings regarding her task, goal, or situation.

  - Does she have a positive sense of well-being or not? Listen to clues in her language; watch her nonverbal body language. (Does she use phrases such as "I have to" or "I get to"? Does she appear defeated, defiant, and defensive or inspired and joyful?)

  - Is the individual experiencing a low quality or high quality of psychological needs? (Does this person feel in control and recognize she has choices, feel supported and have a sense of purpose regarding the situation, and feel she has the ability to navigate the challenges posed by the situation?)

  - Is the individual demonstrating low- or high-quality self-regulation? (Is this person practicing mindfulness, making a values-based decision, or connecting the situation to a higher purpose?)

  - Is the individual's motivational outlook suboptimal (disinterested, external, or imposed) or optimal (aligned, integrated, or inherent)?

- *Facilitate skill 2: Shift to (or maintain) an optimal motivational outlook*—Perhaps the simplest and most direct way to help the individual appreciate his options is to refer to the Spectrum of Motivation model and explore potential upsides and downsides for shifting to a more optimal motivational outlook.

  That shift is most likely to happen through high-quality self-regulation. As a leader, you can facilitate this process through the MVPs:

  - Promote the individual's practice of mindfulness. First, ask for permission to pursue the Power of Why technique. Then as you and the individual discuss the situation, ask a series of questions such as, Why is that important to you? Why do you think that is true for you? Why is that? The question why helps individuals process their situation at a higher level, peeling back layers of distractions that block their awareness of or a link to their psychological needs.

  - Help the individual align the situation with his workplace values. If it hasn't happened in previous sessions, take the time now to help the individual develop workplace values. Ask open-ended questions, recognizing and acknowledging his feelings and emotions. Ultimately, the question you want to ask is, Do you see any alignment between your values and this situation?

  - Help the individual connect the situation to a noble purpose. As with values, if an individual does not have a sense of the purpose of his role, how he contributes to a greater good, or how he serves a higher cause, this is a good time to have the conversation. People will rarely experience an integrated motivational outlook without having a deeply felt, overarching reason that gives meaning to the role they play in a bigger context of work and life.

- *Facilitate skill 3: Reflect*—Guide the individual through a reflection on the outlook conversation experience. What was helpful, awkward, challenging, and enlightening? If the individual experienced a shift to an optimal motivational outlook, inquire how she feels. What is different and why? If no shift occurred and the individual remains in a suboptimal motivational outlook, inquire how she feels. Listen without judgment. Practice mindfulness.

    "Trust the process" may sound trite, but it is true. At their core, people want to be optimally motivated. They naturally gravitate to what is best for them and others when you use the three skills for activating optimal motivation in an authentic, and dare we say it, loving manner.

Close

When do you close an outlook conversation? If you are practicing mindfulness, you will notice when the individual is running low on the emotional energy required to continue examining, exploring, or shifting. When you are not attached to your outcomes or expectations you will be more aware of what the individual is experiencing in the moment. You need to know when enough is enough—for both the individual and yourself! Sometimes you might need to say, "I think you deserve more of my attention and energy than I can give you right now. Are you open to setting up another meeting?"

When you close, seek commitment from the individual to maintain his chosen motivational outlook or continue his examination, identification, and choice of a motivational outlook.

Discuss how the individual might practice high-quality self-regulation and satisfy his psychological needs. Schedule maintenance conversations.

Recognize that when the individual chooses to engage in future outlook conversations with you, he experiences autonomy; your demonstration of support elevates his experience of relatedness; and using the three skills to facilitate an outlook conversation builds the individual's own skill for shifting his motivational outlook any time he chooses, building his sense of competence.

After closing the outlook conversation, you need to reflect. How do you feel about the outlook conversation? Do you have a positive sense of well-being or not? Why? Where were you challenged? Did you have to bite your tongue to stop yourself from jumping into problem solving? Why? How did you manage not to problem solve? Did you act on your own values by staying focused on the individual's needs and not your own? Were you able to practice mindfulness?

Reflective self-examination is a major opportunity to grow as a leader. When we reach out to help others through outlook conversations it is fascinating how much we learn about ourselves.

Blair's Outlook Conversation Turnaround

Blair is a retail manager in an upscale department of a popular department store chain. She also happens to be my niece. One evening Blair excused herself from our dinner to take a call from the head of her department to discuss her intention to write up Randy, one of the department's perennial top salespeople. When Blair returned to dinner, she was obviously upset as she explained how a once-fruitful relationship had deteriorated.

She had explicitly outlined expectations for the staff to promote an upcoming sales event through personal calls and e-mails to their regular customers. When Blair followed up with Randy, he had failed to make any calls. I asked her how she handled that conversation, given that she had knowledge of the principles in this book. "I did what you always recommend. I had an outlook conversation with Randy. I asked why he hadn't made any calls. He told me he hated making phone calls, he couldn't find a quiet place to make the calls, and he felt awkward promoting a sales event to his wealthy clients who have the money to buy items at full price."

Blair is an excellent and natural listener, so I could picture her patiently noting Randy's rationale. She told me how she identified his imposed motivational outlook and proceeded to facilitate his shift to a more optimal outlook.

"I gave him every chance to shift," she told me, "but he still didn't want to make the calls. I am disappointed with the outlook conversation and so frustrated with Randy that I am writing him up. There are times when it is necessary for people to pay the consequences for their failure to perform or for insubordination. This might be that time for Randy."

I asked Blair to describe her process for facilitating Randy's shift. She said, "I told Randy when I am asked to do things I don't like doing, I remember that I chose this profession because of my love for design and fashion. I shared how exciting it is to sell pieces of art that people wear. I told him I value keeping my customers abreast of happenings in our department—treating them like part of our family because that is how I feel. I told him how our clients deserve to learn from the expertise he has gained from his training and years in the industry. I reminded him that he loves this industry, our store, and our customers, too."

After hearing Blair's description, I asked her, "What are Randy's values?" She stared at me for a moment as she had her aha moment. She didn't know what Randy's values were. "It was all about me, wasn't it? About my values, my love for what we do, and my perceptions of what I think Randy should value. I told Randy how I thought his autonomy, relatedness, and competence needs should be satisfied but never gave him a chance to figure it out for himself."

Blair grabbed her cell phone, called her manager, and announced she would not proceed with Randy's disciplinary action. "I have been talked off the cliff," she explained. "I want to try another strategy before punishing Randy for not acting on my instructions."

Curious, I asked Blair what she had hoped to gain by writing up Randy in the first place. Just my asking the question helped Blair realize she had resorted to the "stick" to "motivate" Randy. The stick *would* motivate Randy, but not as she intended. There was a good chance that disciplining Randy for his refusal to make phone calls would deepen his already suboptimal motivational outlook, guaranteeing he would quit and move to a competitor—or worse, would quit and stay.

Another learning for Blair was how focusing on the means Randy took to achieve his goal, rather than the goal itself, had limited his possibilities for successfully doing what they both wanted for him—enhancing client relationships and increasing sales. Blair's reflection led to a realization that Randy did *not* have a suboptimal motivational outlook for selling; he had a suboptimal outlook for making phone calls to promote a sales event. Not only had she imposed her values on Randy, but from there she had jumped into problem-solving Randy's excuses for not making the calls. She also missed an opportunity to bring the real goal into focus—increasing sales by providing customer service and information about a sale—paving the way for creative alternatives.

I can happily report that Blair has become skilled in outlook conversations. She facilitated me in one before I realized what was happening. I experience profound joy when my student becomes the teacher.

Motivational Outlook Conversation with Sonny: The Power of Why

This is an example of a short outlook conversation conducted in a workshop with a young man named Sonny after he challenged the results of a group activity. The purpose of the activity was to demonstrate why it is important to communicate your motivational needs to your manager. After all, managers are not mind readers. Sonny felt at odds with the members of his group, who identified their number one motivator as "interesting work." He was the only one in his group who ranked "money" as his number one motivator.

Sonny explained his stand: "I know this research implies that money is not the best reason to be motivated, but to be honest, it's my reason and I'm not going to apologize for it."

Sonny did not know about the Spectrum of Motivation or the six motivational outlooks, but based on his reaction to the activity and his comment, it seemed an opportune moment to experiment with the Power of Why technique.[4] With Sonny's permission, I conducted the outlook conversation in front of the group.

Susan: Sonny, there are no right or wrong answers. I am hoping you feel curious about the difference in the rankings rather than feel judged. You claim that money is what gets you up to go to work every day. No one else in your group had money as his or her number one motivator. Would you be open to investigating that?

Sonny: Sure.

Susan: Okay, then I am going to ask you a series of questions to explore your motivation. If it gets to be too much, just let me know. Why is money what gets you going each day?

Sonny: I just graduated from college and I'm broke. I need money! That's why I went into sales—to make money.

Susan: That's understandable. Why is the money so important to you?

Sonny: Because I need to buy things!

Susan: Why is buying things so important to you?

Sonny: Because I need things, like a new car.

Susan: Why is the new car so important?

Sonny: Because the one I have now is old and run down. It doesn't scream success. I need a new car to impress people.

Susan: Why is it so important for you to impress people?

Sonny: Because I want them to see me as successful.

Susan: Why is it so important for people to see you as successful?

Sonny paused and, full of emotion, shared that he was the first and only person from his family to ever attend and graduate from college. His parents had sacrificed and worked multiple jobs to support him through those four years. He wanted to be successful as a testament to their sacrifice and caring. I asked questions to clarify whether Sonny was feeling an imposed or aligned motivational outlook, such as, Do you think the reason your parents supported your college education was so you could make lots of money? Do you think your parents have expectations tied to your making a lot of money? Do you think your parents will be disappointed if you don't make a lot of money? Do you think your parents might love you less if you didn't make lots of money?

This is when Sonny got it. He realized that *his interpretation of success* was making lots of money. But his real goal was not making lots of money. The real reason he worked hard every day was out of gratitude for parents who had so selflessly given to him, out of an appreciation for the opportunities before him. It was not about payback, obligation, or duty. It was about relatedness.

A big aha for Sonny was that the money and car he wanted might be by-products. He still wanted them! But he got in touch with how doing meaningful work tied to important values and a noble purpose was a far more rewarding reason for getting out of bed each day. Sonny wondered aloud, What would get him up after he got the car? He concluded that love was more fulfilling than grasping for "things."

Asking someone—including yourself—the question why is a mindfulness tool. This shifting technique peels away the layers of distractions and junk-food urges to connect people to the heart of their motivation—their psychological needs for autonomy, relatedness, and competence.

Motivational Outlook Conversation with Simon: Linking to Values and Purpose

Brash, cocky, twenty-something Simon was complaining to his work group about an assignment to reconfigure the plant's scheduling system. It was obvious from his tone that just talking about the assignment eroded his sense of well-being.

Further examination revealed he didn't have a perception of autonomy. He reported that he had no choice in the matter—the task was delegated to him. Nor did he have a sense of relatedness—he felt taken advantage of since the task was not part of his job description or what he considered to be the purpose of his role. He was assigned the scheduling because of his expertise in computer programming and operational systems. Even though Simon was competent, his psychological need for competence was not being satisfied. He resented that his manager delegated a task to him because he was the only one with the competence to do it.

Little self-regulation was going on. Simon seemed to be reveling in his self-righteous indignation. He thought he had a right to be ticked off. From what I could tell, he was gaining a lot of energy from the junk-food diet of anger and resentment. He had little interest in shifting to a healthier motivational outlook, which might have signaled he was in the disinterested motivational outlook. But his defiant energy exposed his imposed motivational outlook.

At this point in our conversation, I asked Simon if he would be willing to engage in a values discussion. Was he comfortable sharing his personal values and how they relate to his work? One thing was true about Simon: he appreciated a challenge. I think he was looking for a fight. That meant I needed high-quality self-regulation as the facilitator of the outlook conversation. "Practice mindfulness," I reminded myself.

Simon was clear and articulate about his values. As many of his generation will tell you, his time outside of work is precious to him. He witnessed how his parents' dedication to work and loyalty to organizations had ended with layoffs. Simon is a member of a generation clearly not interested in the surging divorce rates, heightened substance abuse, and physical and mental distress that plagued their parents' generation.[5]

It turned out that the pivotal question for Simon was, "Do you see any link between the scheduling project you have been assigned and your values?" People sitting behind him reported that as soon as I asked the question, Simon's posture changed. Even without being able to see his face, they sensed a shift in energy. The rest of us watched a slow smile form on Simon's face as he conceded, "Okay, that's cool." He went on to admit that the scheduling project was aligned with two important values. First, the scheduling system would make time at work more efficient, allowing him more precious time outside of work. Second, he valued being a team player. By applying his expertise to a more efficient scheduling system, he would be giving the gift of more efficient time to his team members as well.

Within a few minutes, Simon's perspective had shifted from an imposed motivational outlook to an aligned motivational outlook. What I found even more fascinating was how his entire demeanor changed regarding his learning and participation during the rest of the session. Motivational outlooks are contagious—for bad or for good, depending on the outlook. In Simon's case, his shift created a positive ripple effect appreciated by the entire group.

You will notice that I avoided the problem-solving pit-fall. If you were Simon's manager who delegated him the job of redesigning the plant's scheduling system, you might have noticed Simon's procrastination and decided to dis-cuss it with him. In the meeting, Simon makes all kinds of excuses—the delegated assignment is not part of his job description, he doesn't have time, he doesn't have the resources, and on and on. With good intentions, you might facilitate problem solving by asking thought-provoking questions and generating thoughtful alternatives.

No matter how solid your solutions and action plans are, one basic fact remains: Simon does not want to do the project. He has an imposed motivational outlook with low-quality energy, vitality, and well-being. Until you deal with Simon's motivational outlook, your problem-solving seeds fall on uncultivated soil.

As a first step, you may need to work with your staff to develop and clarify their individual work-related values and purpose. Then, when you conduct a motivational outlook conversation, you will be more likely to facilitate a shift by helping them make the connection between their task, goal, or situation and their developed values and sense of purpose.

Here is the point about outlook conversations: you don't know where they will go or how people will connect with their psychological needs. As the facilitator, you need to be open to the process and trust that when people are able to use high-quality self-regulation (they are mindful, val-ues based, and purposeful), they experience high-quality psychological needs (they satisfy their needs for autonomy, relatedness, and competence). Then, more often than not, they come to conclusions that not only generate positive energy, vitality, and a sense of well-being for them but also consider the welfare of the whole.

Office Maneuvers

In the opening scenario of this chapter, the manager asked her team member to give up his office space. He said no, he wasn't willing to give up what he worked so hard to earn. The manager took responsibility for the decision, believing she had tried to take away one of his prime motivators—his status. She concluded that the team member was not motivated to give up his office space.

What if the manager had facilitated an outlook conversation to help the team member sort through his feelings on the topic? She could have helped him clarify his individual goals and the team's interdependent goals, explore his values related to being a team member, and examine his connection to the team's noble purpose. What if she had used the Power of Why to help him better understand if his psychological needs were being satisfied through his status—or not.

Maybe an outlook conversation could have helped the team member discover that it wasn't status he was fighting for but a sense of fairness.

The office was a symbol, obviously. The manager interpreted the office as a status symbol, but it could also have been a symbol of justice. At a deeper level, the office could have represented appreciation and caring. The request to give up his office could have been tugging at the team member's sense of relatedness—which is the opposite of what status does. Status is a power-up position that undermines relatedness in both the person in power and the people in the lower positions.

What if the team member's relatedness needs had been better understood? Maybe he would have participated in a brainstorming session about the team's goals and the resources needed to meet those goals. Realizing that his opinion and input mattered, he may have determined there was a better use of his office and offered it as a solution. That proactive gesture might have helped him feel good about himself and elevated the team's appreciation of him. With an outlook conversation, his manager could have helped make shift happen.

Motivation Mini Case Study: Walter's First Time

My hope is that you are optimally motivated to making shift happen by facilitating outlook conversations. But you might be wondering where and how to begin. That was the question facing Walter after attending a skill-building session in Europe. He decided to send out a message to his team members explaining that he needed to practice conducting outlook conversations. He asked them to contact him if they were struggling with motivation at work.

Walter didn't know whether to be glad or sad when he received eight responses. His first outlook conversation was challenging, but as he reported, "We both had a good feeling about it. It helps the thinking process. I prepared for the session by composing an opening statement. I then briefly explained the Spectrum of Motivation model. I dedicated the most time to identifying the team member's motivational outlook before using the Power of Why. I found myself needing to focus and practice mindfulness. At one point, she started asking *me* the *why* questions! We took the final fifteen minutes to review."

In the spirit of confidentiality, Walter didn't share specific content or the name of the team member, but he did tell me that she requested a follow-up conversation. She told Walter how much she appreciated the deep conversation—the first time somebody had tried to understand her complex thoughts and emotions. It turns out this valuable employee had been on the verge of quitting but was renewed by the sense of relatedness generated by her team leader. Not bad for Walter's inaugural outlook conversation!

Recapping "Making Shift Happen"

Leadership is not a role; leadership is a practice. One does not just assume a role as a doctor, attorney, CPA, musician, or artist. One practices medicine, law, accounting, music, or art. Great leadership takes great practice. When it comes to motivation, leadership practice includes being a role model by applying the three skills of activating motivation to your own tasks, goals, and situations. When you practice leadership, you invest the emotional labor required to observe what your people are *experiencing*, how they are *feeling*, and *why*—and then discuss it with them. The best approach for having that conversation is facilitating a motivational outlook conversation. When you help people *identify* their current motivational outlook, help them *shift* to an optimal motivational outlook, and ask open-ended questions to help them *reflect*, you are practicing sophisticated leadership that makes a meaningful difference.

Before you can successfully lead someone through a conversation to discuss that person's motivation, however, you must prepare by assuring *you* have an optimal motivational outlook regarding the individual, the topic, and the commitment necessary for facilitating the conversation. Devoting time and effort to help people shift their motivational outlook pays off in countless ways for them, your organization, and you as a leader. But the skill needed to reap these rewards may require more than practice. It may require a change in basic beliefs about doing business, which happens to be the topic tackled in chapter 6.

6.

Rethinking Five Beliefs That Erode Workplace Motivation

Motivation is one of the most vital and essential aspects of leadership and one of the most confused and misunderstood. The result of this confusion and misunderstanding is leaders who have become blind to what does and doesn't work. They engage in counterproductive behaviors believing they are doing the right thing. Leaders are so immersed in five motivation-eroding beliefs that they find it difficult to hear, see, or do something different.

Research over the past sixty years continues to prove the point. Individuals' rankings of workplace motivators are compared to rankings of what their managers think motivates them. The results reflect how most individuals feel: managers simply do not know what motivates their people. Managers tend to attribute external motivation to employees (actions not within the employees' control)—such as good wages, promotions, and job security. On the other hand, employees prefer more internal motivation (actions within the employees' control)—such as interesting work, growth, and learning.[1]

Why the big disconnect? One reason is that leaders do not have access to someone else's internal state of motivation, only their own. That probably explains why managers tend to attribute internal motivations to themselves at the same time they judge others to be externally motivated. However, when it comes to their employees, leaders depend on their observations of external behaviors and conditions to evaluate their employees' motivation. Unfortunately, many leaders are not perceptive observers, nor are they wise interpreters of what they see. It is nearly impossible for a leader to understand others' internal state of motivation by observing their external behavior. (This is another good reason why conducting motivational outlook conversations is so important.)

To make it more confounding, as I have pointed out throughout this book, different people can internalize the same conditions differently. For example, in a team meeting where all the members are asked to share personal information, you will find all six motivational outlooks being played out. The leader needs to find ways of shaping the request and the environment so that people might choose an optimal, rather than a suboptimal, motivational outlook.

Research suggests that another reason for the disconnect in the ranking of motivators between employees and their managers is that employees don't understand the true nature of their own motivation. For example, an employee who feels trapped in her job, feels she is being taken advantage of, or feels overwhelmed by what is being asked of her may ask for more money. Under her breath, she is saying, "They don't pay me enough to put up with this." What she doesn't understand is that there will never be enough money to make up for the void created when her psychological needs for autonomy, relatedness, and competence are not satisfied. People can't ask for what they don't know they need.

When leaders and their employees attribute their workplace dissatisfaction to money or external factors, it sets up a series of erroneous assumptions and detrimental actions. First, even though people need and want money and external rewards, believing those will make them happy distracts them from what actually does make them happy. Second, it lets leaders, who typically don't have direct control over pay raises and rewards, off the motivational hook. They throw their arms up in a leadership mea culpa and declare there's nothing they can do. Leaders may also use their lack of control over salaries and benefits as an excuse to avoid dealing with people's emotionally charged discontent. Third, when people use external motivators as the reason for their dissatisfaction in the workplace, it perpetuates outdated beliefs that lead to ineffective motivational leadership.

The primary purpose of this chapter is to explore the third phenomenon—how your unexplored leadership beliefs could be influencing, and maybe even sabotaging, your approach to motivation.

Dr. David Facer began researching leaders' beliefs about what motivates employees because he sees motivation as not only an employee well-being issue but also a strategic one. "The innovation that leaders, especially senior leaders, ask from employees to make the firm more competitive and valuable is the result of a delicate creative process. I am endlessly curious how leaders explain the mixed outcomes that their pressure and the standard incentive programs generate. Go listen to employees talking at Starbucks. As plain as day they're telling us they want a different approach."

A different, long-term approach will require a belief change, David says, but leaders are seldom asked to examine their beliefs. To make that examination easier, he created and validated the Motivation Beliefs Inventory, a short survey that consultants and executive coaches can use to help leaders consciously examine their motivation beliefs—and try on new ones. David is convinced that too many leaders do not understand how their underlying motivational beliefs shape the problems they face. He says, "The negative evidence is too compelling to ignore. Employees are craving fresh approaches to motivation that make it much easier for them to rise to the innovation challenge."[2]

In the introduction to this book, I posed unfinished belief statements and asked you to consider how to fill in the blanks. Here they are again, as a reminder:

1. It's not personal; it's just _____.

2. The purpose of business is to _____.

3. Leaders are in a position of _____.

4. The only thing that really matters is _____.

5. If you cannot measure it, it _____.

These are particularly sticky beliefs that erode workplace motivation. Have you thought about where these common beliefs come from? They are so entrenched in organizational consciousness that we accept them without question. I have yet to find a leader who couldn't complete most, if not all, of the belief statements. This poses a potential problem. Unexplored beliefs become the foundation for programmed values. Then these programmed values become the basis for rules, processes, procedures, actions, and your leadership behaviors.

Your mission, should you choose to accept it, is to explore these workplace beliefs and examine how they tend to undermine your people's optimal motivation and then consider alternative beliefs and best practices. I encourage you to shine a light on potentially unexamined values in the spirit of developing more meaningful motivational leadership values.

Rethink the First Eroding Belief: It's Not Personal; It's Just Business

Employees probably spend more of their waking hours connected to work and interacting with their coworkers than with family members. Yet managers believe their actions are not personal and just business.

Every day you deliver information, feedback, or news to those you lead that affects their work, livelihood, opportunities, status, income, mood, health, or well-being. How is this not personal?

Whatever your beliefs, one thing is true: what you say and do *feels* personal to the people you lead! Therein lies the issue: *feelings*. Earlier in this book we explored the issue of the f-word in organizations. Do you believe that expressing feelings does not belong in the workplace? If so, challenge yourself by asking, How did this belief become so commonly held? Where did *my* belief come from?

One possibility why feelings are discouraged in the workplace is that managers do not have the skill to effectively deal with them. True, some employees do not self-regulate well and may let their emotions get the best of them from time to time. But the fear of unruly emotions is disproportionate to the occurrence and severity of emotional outbreaks.

What if you changed the belief that it's not personal, it's just business to one more likely to activate optimal motivation? *If it is business, it is personal.*

Try embracing the idea that all emotions are acceptable but not all behavior is acceptable. Notice, acknowledge, and deal with a person's emotions. Practice self-regulation by listening to your heart and acknowledging the crucial role that feelings play in your work and life.

Consider letting go of leadership practices that undermine people's psychological needs and adopt best practices that encourage them. As your beliefs change, watch how your leadership practices change—and how your people respond.[3]

What Doesn't Work	What Does Work
Think to yourself or tell a person directly, "You shouldn't feel that way."	Acknowledge and validate people's feelings and emotions.
Be judgmental and make approval conditional.	Offer pure or descriptive feedback rather than evaluative feedback or personalized praising.
Tolerate sabotaging actions or unacceptable patterns of behavior.	Facilitate the Generation of options and ask open-ended questions to promote mindfulness.

Rethink the Second Eroding Belief:
The Purpose of Business Is to Make Money

When you hold the belief that making money is the purpose of business, you are likely to focus on dashboard metrics instead of focusing on the people responsible for providing quality service to your customers and clients. You are apt to overemphasize results and resort to pressuring people to get those results. You may be tempted to employ questionable ethical practices. When given a choice, you might choose quantity over quality, short-term results over long-term results, and profits over people.

Consider how an alternative belief would generate a different approach to your leadership. How would your decisions and actions be different if they were based on the following belief: *The purpose of business is to serve.*

Think how this reframed belief might alter your organization's dashboard metrics—or at least the content and quality of the goals. How might reframing the goals so they focus on internal as well as external service, the quality of people's efforts as well as the results of their efforts, or learning and growth in addition to accomplishments change the way you lead day to day?

Hard-nosed businesspeople will push back on these ideas with a traditional argument: "You can serve all you want, but this soft stuff doesn't make you money, and if you don't make a profit, you will go out of business. Then you won't be serving anyone."

Yes, a business must make a profit to sustain itself. But it is an illogical leap to conclude that profit is therefore the purpose of business. You need air to live, plus water and food. But the purpose of your life is not to just breathe, drink, and eat. Your purpose is richer and more profound than basic survival. The more noble your purpose and developed your values are, the more they influence *how* you live day to day.

The nature of human motivation is not about making money. The nature of human motivation is in making meaning.

Making a profit or serving your people who serve your customers is never an either-or decision. It is always both. But service comes before profit. To paraphrase what I have often heard Ken Blanchard proclaim, "Profit is the applause you get from creating an optimally motivating environment for your people so they want to take care of your customers." Definitive evidence shows that organizational vitality measured by return on investment, earnings by share, access to venture capital, stock price, debt load, and other financial indicators is dependent on two factors: employee work passion and customer devotion. It does not work the other way around—organizational vitality is *not* what determines customer devotion or employee work passion.[4]

When you focus on satisfying your employees' psychological needs so they can serve customers' needs, your organization prospers. An old sports analogy works equally well in business: focusing on profit is like playing the game with your eye on the scoreboard instead of the ball.

Challenge the belief that the purpose of business is to make money, and consider an optimal motivation belief: *the purpose of business is to serve—both your people and*

your customers. Profit is a by-product of doing both of these well.

Watch how your people respond to your changed belief. When you believe that the purpose of business is to *serve*, you lead differently. Your decisions and actions are more likely to cultivate a workplace that supports people's optimal motivation. Then notice the results and accept the well-earned applause in the form of organizational vitality. Keep that in mind as you avoid practices that undermine people's psychological needs and adopt best practices to encourage them.[5]

What Doesn't Work	What Does Work
Drive profit at the expense of people.	Help individuals align to work-related values and a sense of purpose. Frame actions in terms of the welfare of the whole.
Delay skill-related feedback or punish lack of competence.	Provide an honest assessment of skills and training needs.
See people as tireless machines.	Clear time for inherently motivating projects.

Rethink the Third Eroding Belief: Leaders Are in a Position of Power

Imagine you work for a large organization. You catch th elevator to another floor and notice someone is alrea in it—the company's CEO. You have never met him, k you recognize him from company-wide meetings. Yo

heart might race a bit. You might think twice before you speak. You might feel excited at the opportunity to make his acquaintance, or you might feel worried about making a bad impression. Suffice it to say, if he was someone of lesser stature or if you hadn't recognized him as the CEO, the dynamic would be different.

"Managers need to be incredibly mindful and clear about the types of power they have and use. Most leaders will be surprised by the potentially negative emotional impact that results from having and using their power, in almost all its forms." These are the words of Dr. Drea Zigarmi, who found himself surprised by the strength of his own research on how a leader's power affects people's motivational outlooks.[6] Even when you don't have intentions to use your power, just having it creates a dynamic that requires your awareness and sensitivity.

Drea and his colleagues studied the use of power by leaders in the workplace. You might find it helpful to consider the most commonly used types of power described below and the potential effect each one has on your people's emotional well-being, intentions, and motivational outlooks. What you discover might surprise you.

- *Reward power* is your power to promise monetary or nonmonetary compensation. There are two types of reward power:

  - *Impersonal reward power* is the power to grant special benefits, promotions, or favorable considerations

  - *Personal reward power* is the power you have when your employees' feelings depend on being accepted, valued, and liked by you.

Employees report that when they perceive either form of reward power at work, they experience a suboptimal motivational outlook.

• *Coercive power* is your power to use threats and punishment if people fail to conform to desired outcomes. Understandably, the use of coercive power usually results in a negative relationship between leader and follower—and a suboptimal motivational outlook. Leaders often see coercive power as the easiest, most expedient, and most justifiable form of power. Truly the junk food of power, coercive power creates a workplace where people need to consciously exercise high-quality self-regulation to avoid a suboptimal motivational outlook.

• *Referent power* is based on how your employees identify with you. Ironically, you may enjoy certain work relationships because your employees' self-identity is enhanced through interaction with you, their actions are based on their desire to be similar to and associated with you, or they think so highly of you that they are afraid to disagree with you. It might surprise you to discover that when employees report that their managers have referent power, they also report experiencing a suboptimal motivational outlook. Their dependence on you for their internal state of well-being tends to undermine their autonomy, relatedness, and competence.

• *Legitimate power* is bestowed through a position or title that gives a leader the justifiable right to request compliance from another individual. Having legitimate power is a blessing and a curse. With it, you can do more good, but, as Spider-Man will tell you, "With great power comes great responsibility." You must be sensitive to how others perceive and integrate your legitimate power, lest, despite your good intentions, people interpret your power as diminishing their experience of ARC. Often referred to as *position power*, legitimate power is manifest in a variety of forms.

- *Reciprocity* is the power stemming from your employees feeling obligated to comply with your requests because you have done something positive for them.

- *Equity power*, thought of as quid pro quo, is the power you have when an employee senses that you expect some type of compensation for the work or the effort you have put into the relationship.

- *Dependence power* is the power you have when your employees feel obliged to assist you because you're in need—not out of a sense of relatedness but from an imposed sense of social responsibility.

- *Expert power* is power that comes through your depth and breadth of knowledge. Expert power relies on the perceptions your employees hold regarding your superior knowledge.

- *Information power* relies on your employees' perception on how you present persuasive material or logic.

Even these last two types of power can result in employees reporting a suboptimal motivational outlook when they feel manipulated, threatened, or overwhelmed by your expertise or use of information (knowledge or power).

The bottom line is that power undermines people's psychological needs. It's not just your use of the power; it's people's perception that you *have it* and *could use it*. Your power demands that people need to exert more energy self-regulating to internalize a workplace where they experience autonomy, relatedness, and competence. As Drea puts it, "Power is very precious stuff. It entices the leader into flights of self-delusion and separateness from those they lead."[7]

If you are the CEO riding the elevator, by virtue of your title and assumed power, you are not wielding power, but *having* power changes the dynamic between you and the people you lead. So what is a leader to do?

When Dr. Ken Blanchard was elected class president in the seventh grade, his father congratulated him and then told him, "Now that you have power, don't ever use it. Great leaders are great because people trust and respect them, not because they have power." Theodore Blanchard was an admiral in the navy who told Ken that anyone who thinks that military-style leadership is my-way-or-the-highway leadership has never gone to battle. According to Admiral Blanchard, "If leaders acted like that, your men would shoot you before the enemy could."

You can use all your power attempting to motivate people, but it won't work if you want them to experience an optimal motivational outlook. Shifting to an optimal motivational outlook is something people can do only for themselves. But the workplace you create has an enormous influence on how likely—or challenging—it is for people to self-regulate, satisfy their psychological needs for ARC, and experience optimal motivation.

We need to change the belief that leaders are in a position of power. Consider the difference with an optimal motivation belief. *Leaders are in a position of creating a workplace where people are more likely to satisfy their psychological needs for ARC.*

When you avoid undermining practices and adopt best practices, you focus your power on cultivating a workplace where your people, your organization, and you, are reaping the rewards of optimal motivation.[8]

What Doesn't Work	What Does Work
Apply pressure and demand accountability.	Invite choice. Explore options within boundaries.
Rely on your position or coercive power.	Explore individuals' natural interest in and enthusiasm for the goal.
Withhold or hide your reasoning behind decisions.	Provide a rationale and share information. Discuss your intentions openly.

Rethink the Fourth Eroding Belief: The Only Thing That Really Matters Is Results

At a recent speaking engagement, I asked, "How would you finish this statement: The only thing that really matters in business is *blank*?" The answer was so obvious that over three hundred people spontaneously filled in the blank by yelling in unison, "Results!"

I then asked them to consider the effect this tyranny of results has on the workplace. It was not easy. Leaders tend to tune out as soon as you mess with results. Executives cannot imagine what matters at the end of the day besides results measured by dashboard metrics. I'm asking you what I asked of them—to consider three alternatives to the traditional results focus.

Option 1: Redefine and reframe results

People want to achieve organizational metrics and assigned goals (when they are fair and agreed upon), but often internalize them as external or imposed. You can help people shift to an aligned motivational outlook by clarifying the underlying values behind your dashboard metrics. People may even shift to an integrated motivational outlook when metrics are authentically positioned as a means to fulfilling a noble purpose.

When Express Employment Professionals announced sales goals at a recent conference of franchise owners, the leaders reminded the attendees that the purpose of their business is to put a million people to work. The energy generated was electric! When Berrett-Koehler, my publisher, puts out its catalog of offerings to buyers, the cover's primary message is "A community dedicated to creating a world that works for all." My experience has been that every goal, metric, and decision pursued at Berrett-Koehler has that purpose at heart. When I received a detailed production schedule, I no longer perceived deadlines as imposed "dreadlines" but rather as helpful guidelines enabling each of us to do our part. This is my sixth book but my first with Berrett-Koehler. I have never been as optimally motivated to meet deadlines!

Framing results differently and trusting that individuals will still achieve necessary metrics will help people shift their motivational outlook.

Option 2: Set high-quality goals

Research shows that leaders need to help their people avoid potentially external goals such as

- Social recognition, such as increasing the number of friends or contacts to improve social or professional status

- Image and appearance, such as losing weight to look good at a reunion or to be more attractive

- Material success, such as earning more money, buying a luxury car, or moving to a prestigious neighborhood[9]

Instead, leaders need to help individuals set goals that promote more optimal motivational outlooks, including

- Personal growth, such as improving listening skills or practicing mindfulness

- Affiliation, such as nurturing a mentoring relationship or enhancing working relationships with others

- Community, such as contributing to something bigger than yourself, or making a difference

- Physical health, such as losing weight as a means for increasing energy or changing your eating habits as a way of lowering blood pressure[10]

There is a real and meaningful difference between these two goals:

- If you eat well, you are more likely to be physically appealing and look younger at a later age.
- If you eat well, you are more likely to be fit and remain healthy at a later age.

Applied to a business setting, consider the real and meaningful difference in the expression of these two goals:

- If you make your numbers, you are more likely to be in the President's Club and qualify for the reward trip.
- If you make your numbers, you are more likely to be solving your clients' problems and making a difference.

Individuals will benefit from higher-quality goals. Setting such goals is also a way to shift from results to meaningful results.

The quality of goals your people set determines the quality of their experience. The values behind the goal determine the value of the goal.

Option 3: Do not imply that ends justify the means

If you believe results are what really matter without considering *why* those results are meaningful and *how* people go about achieving them, you are in essence saying the ends justify the means. What a sorry picture this paints. We do not need the science of motivation to prove that means matter. We witness the scandals and horror stories of people, organizations, industries, and countries who prize ends over means every day in the news.

A graphic illustration is captured in the Academy Award–nominated 2005 documentary *Enron: The Smartest Guys in the Room*. You could read the book upon which it is based, but then you wouldn't hear the unnerving taped conversations between giddy energy brokers celebrating as California is ravaged by fires and people are losing everything they own—and their lives. The brokers knew the fires would spark higher energy demands and prices, ensuring the results for which they were being held accountable.

Enron is considered one of the ugliest business scandals in American history. But it is more disturbing as an example of what happens when people prize results more than the means to achieve them. You ache for those who suffered at the hands of the energy brokers but also for the brokers themselves who were addicted to motivational junk food so unhealthy it poisoned their morals. The brokers have responsibility for their own actions, which is why I think every individual should learn the skill of optimal motivation. However, the leaders were also responsible for creating a culture based on beliefs that eroded autonomy, relatedness, and competence—and led to inhumane behavior.

A focus on results may yield short-term gains. However, those gains are at risk and compromised when people feel pressure instead of autonomy, disconnection instead of relatedness, and a sense of being used without a sense of the competence they have gained.

The evidence is clear: people *can* achieve the results you want, even if their psychological needs are thwarted in the process. But their negative energy and lack of well-being make it rare for them to sustain or repeat those results—let alone exceed them.

Reframe the belief that the only thing that matters is results. Consider an optimal motivation belief instead. *In the end, what really matters is not just the results people achieve but why and how people achieve them.*

Observe the shift in people's energy—and your own—when you focus on what really matters in the workplace. Focus on *meaningful* results that satisfy people's psychological needs for optimal motivation. Then trust that the numbers will add up.[11]

What Doesn't Work	What Does Work
Impose goals and deadlines.	Present goals and timelines as valuable information necessary for accomplishing agreed-upon outcomes. Help individuals reframe goals so they are meaningful to them while still achieving the outcomes required.
Focus on the needs of the organization without equal attention to the needs of the individuals you lead.	Provide individuals the appropriate direction and support needed for their level of development.
Evaluate output while ignoring effort.	Explore alternatives for stimulating implementation strategies.

Rethink the Fifth Eroding Belief: If You Cannot Measure It, It Doesn't Matter

I was a longtime aficionado of SMART goal setting when the *M* stood for *Measurable*. However, over time, I found that a specific, measurable, attainable, relevant, and time-bound goal simply was not SMART enough. I changed the *M* to *Motivating* and moved *measurable* into the *S* (*Specific*). Adding another dimension to make my goals more emotionally compelling worked for me. It seemed to work for others, too. Now the science of motivation explains why.

The nature of things that cannot be measured

Setting measurable goals and outcomes is important. Having a defined finish line in front of you can be positively compelling. Previously, I encouraged leaders and individuals to ensure a higher level of results by reframing *measurable* goals into *meaningful* goals. However, we need to move beyond SMART goal setting and embrace aspects of work that are not easily measured.

Case in point: if you are a parent, you probably have SMART goals for your child's education and acquisition of skills. But how would you answer this question: What do you most hope for your child? Most parents tell me they hope their children experience meaningful relationships, enjoy a profound connection to the world, contribute to society, give and receive love, fulfill a noble purpose, are passionate about their work, discover what makes them happy, feel safe and secure, perceive they have choices, and are able to navigate and master the world around them.

The dreams parents most hope for their children cannot be easily measured. I find the same phenomenon happens when I ask leaders what they most hope for their people at work. They may use different terms, but what they want for their people is a positive sense of well-being. At the heart of what leaders hope for their people is the satisfaction of their psychological needs for autonomy, relatedness, and competence. Despite the deep knowledge that what they really want for people are the benefits that come through these emotionally compelling aspects of work, leaders still continue to focus attention on what they can easily measure.

As in life, the most rewarding aspects of work are those most difficult to measure.

If you believe the statement "If you cannot measure it, it does not matter," ask yourself why. Is dealing with the emotional nature of things not easily measured outside your comfort zone? Do you believe your job is to control circumstances and it is difficult to control something that's not easily measured?

Some things are best left unmeasured

One of life's great joys is eating in Italy. Ask anyone who has traveled there—food tastes better in Italy. I had the profound experience of attending a weeklong cooking course in Tuscany. I say "profound" because it literally changed the quality of my life—not just my cooking but also my perspective on day-to-day living. The chef refused to provide exact measurements for anything he made. "How can I tell you how much water to put in the pasta dough? It depends on the quality of your flour and the kind of day—the temperature, the humidity. You must add some water and oil until it feels right." He was also hesitant to commit to a menu or plan for the week. If the zucchini flowers were blossoming, we would have fried squash blossoms; if not, then the ripe tomatoes would become the center-piece of a Caprese salad. The chef was really teaching us mindfulness—to be present in the moment, to notice the world around us and be aware of our many options and choices. The food becomes a possibility for something pro-found. And people can taste the difference.

Reframe the belief that if you cannot measure it, it is not important. Put an optimal motivation belief into practice instead. *If you cannot measure it, it is probably really, really important.*

Of course, we need to measure many things in life and work. Pastries are a science where measuring makes the difference between a fluffy cupcake and a hockey puck. But a true growth step for leaders is to become more mindful of promoting dreams, ideals, and experiences that cannot be easily measured. That includes becoming more comfortable with feelings. If leaders rule out people's emotional nature at work—including their own—because they are not mind-ful or skilled enough to cope, we all lose what it means to be fully human. That is too high a price to pay for being comfortable. Observe the shift in energy when you focus your leadership on promoting what cannot be easily mea-sured—such as love, joy, and gratitude. Your people will eat it up.

Challenge your own comfort zone as you lead with best practices that encourage people's psychological needs.[12]

What Doesn't Work	What Does Work
Overemphasize metrics and competition.	Explore individuals' natural interest in and enthusiasm for the goal.
Underestimate learning. Continually delay or cancel learning and development opportunities and training programs.	Emphasize learning goals, not just performance goals.
Make mistakes a mistake.	Encourage self-reflection and growth. Legitimize mistakes as part of the learning process.

Recapping "Rethinking Five Beliefs That Erode Workplace Motivation"

What has become clear to you about why motivating people doesn't work and what does? My hope is that you are willing to challenge your beliefs, and the values built upon those beliefs, when it comes to motivation.

Do your underlying beliefs and values promote or erode optimal motivation in the workplace?

Not all beliefs are values, but all values are beliefs. The quality of your beliefs determines the quality of your leadership values. Your leadership values ultimately determine how you lead and the quality of the workplace you create.

7.

The Promise of
Optimal Motivation

Being a leader is a privileged position. What you say, how you say it, and why you say it make a difference in the lives of the people you lead.

The Promise of Optimal Motivation for You, as a Leader

David Facer and I ask our executive audiences this question: "What do you want *from* your people?"

We get immediate and reasonable responses, such as "I want their focus, attention, effort, dedication, and loyalty." "I want them to meet expectations, make their numbers, achieve their goals, do what I ask of them, and get results."

Then we ask a follow-up question: "What do you want *for* your people?"

It's funny how removing one letter from the question generates blank, dumbfounded stares on most faces. You see skepticism or even cynicism as they sense you are about to discuss some touchy-feely topic. With some prodding, though, the executives come up with what they want for their people: happiness, safety, security, health, fun, a sense of accomplishment, and peace.

We find these answers fascinating. The responses are very similar to the characteristics of positive well-being listed in chapter 4. Executives tend to pursue results by focusing on what they want from people. They have it backwards.

When you focus on what you want *for* people, you are more likely to get the results you want *from* people.

The Promise of Optimal Motivation for the Organization

Most leaders are stuck with systems that promote driving over thriving. Organizational systems are built on the faulty assumption that people need to be reinforced, rewarded, or driven to accomplish goals. They underestimate people's basic needs to grow, excel, and contribute. People have a basic desire to thrive.

Even with the new science of motivation, many organizations will continue to bank on motivating people through external means that appear expedient, easy, and controllable. The question is, *At what cost?* Escalating salaries, bonuses, and rewards are obvious costs. But when an organization focuses on rewarding the top 10 percent, what does it do to the motivation of the other 90 percent? What about the hidden costs of detrimental mental and physical health, absenteeism, and increased insurance rates, to name a few, wrought by traditional motivation's focus on motivational junk food? What about the opportunity losses in terms of dedication, loyalty, creativity, and innovation?[1]

The time has come to consider the potential *opportunity gains* in teaching leaders and individuals the skill of activating optimal motivation. What might happen if organizations expanded their traditional focus on results, performance, and productivity to focus on helping people satisfy their needs for ARC? What if leaders learned to avoid undermining practices and adopt best practices, including motivational outlook conversations? What if values were developed based on optimal motivation beliefs, rather than outdated traditional beliefs?

Answers to these questions could lead to a workplace where autonomous people hold *themselves* accountable; where meaningful relationships translate into organizational citizenship behaviors; and competence leads to a learning organization rich with innovation, quality products and services, and streamlined processes.

When the ideas in this book move from theory into practice, a workplace full of passionate people with a positive sense of well-being is the opportunity and the promise.

The Promise of Optimal Motivation for the Individuals You Lead

The following personal experience reinforces the difference it makes when you help individuals reframe their motivational experiences.

This would be either Alexa's final game or a trip to the state championship. Her high school volleyball team was playing their crosstown rival for the privilege of representing their division in the playoffs. Anyone who has been involved in high school sports knows it can get tense and exciting—and parents can be more animated than the student athletes. Alexa's dad, Drea, and I were shouting and jumping up with every point. In the best-of-three series, the two teams were tied going into the third game. It was do or die. This was side-out volleyball, meaning that the only way a team could score was during a serve. The server would continue serving until she lost the point. Alexa's team was down and it didn't look good. Then Alexa stepped up to serve. It felt as if I was holding my breath during her entire service.

She won the first point. Then the second. Alexa's team moved ahead and they went on to win the game. Drea and I were beside ourselves! I rushed down the bleachers to celebrate—I flew! Somehow, my husband beat me to Alexa and there he was, doing his Italian dad thing: kissing her on her forehead and hugging her.

I was impatiently awaiting my turn. Finally, Drea stepped back—I thought this was my chance. But with his hands on Alexa's shoulders, he looked her directly in the eyes and asked, "Alexa, when you got up to serve, your team was losing 9 to 12. By the time you finished your serve, your team was ahead 13 to 12 and went on to win the game. How did *you* feel about your serve tonight?"

I rolled my eyes and thought, *Stop talking; let me in there to celebrate!* Then I noticed something I had never witnessed before. Alexa's eyes literally began to glow. She said, "Dad! You know how I hated working out this summer and got so frustrated with my serve and wanted to quit volleyball? Tonight when I hit that overhead slam, I saw movement on the ball and I knew there was no way they could return it. I got into the flow and it was amazing! I am so happy for my team!"

In that moment, I realized the power of activating optimal motivation with others. In his wisdom, Drea first practiced the skill of motivation for himself. Through his own high-quality self-regulation, he made the moment about Alexa and her experience, not his experience. What if I had gotten to Alexa first? I enjoy being excited and celebrating. Our conversation would have been all about me: my excitement, my pleasure, and my interpretation of what just happened. I needed to reflect and ask myself, *Why are you excited? Whose experience are you celebrating?*

Had I gotten to Alexa before Drea, I could have undermined her psychological needs in an attempt to satisfy my own. Drea self-regulated and acted on his love for his daughter. In that moment, he gave her a priceless gift.

Asking Alexa how she felt gave her the gift of *autonomy*— she had the opportunity to reflect on her interpretation of what happened and choose how she would remember it.

Drea gave her the gift of *relatedness*—he obviously cared more about Alexa than his own need to express his excitement. He also gave her the opportunity to relate her great performance to the overall team experience. She realized her excitement wasn't just in winning but in contributing to the team's success.

Drea also gave Alexa the gift of *competence*—for the first time in her teen years, I believe Alexa made the connection between hard work and results, between effort and outcome. She felt masterful in that moment. She will be able to recall and relish that sense of competence for the rest of her life.

Her father created a pocket of tranquility in an atmosphere where it would be easy to think the experience was only about winning. Alexa reflected and rejoiced in a deeper, more profound way. Don't get me wrong—she felt jubilation, but the reasons she felt it shifted. An interaction between a father and daughter reinforced the power of optimal motivation, but the lesson learned is relevant for any workplace.

The Essence of the Promise of Optimal Motivation

A great irony of leadership is that motivating your people doesn't work because people are already motivated. People are always motivated. What does work is helping people understand *why* they are motivated. Your opportunity lies in facilitating people's shift to an optimal motivational outlook so they flourish as they succeed. When you activate optimal motivation for yourself, you provide more than a role model—you create a ripple effect that encourages your people's optimal motivation.

Imagine people choosing to come to work because they experience a sense of positive well-being, the feeling that they are contributing to something greater than themselves, and the thrill of continued growth and learning. *People can flourish as they succeed. This is the promise of optimal motivation.*

• Afterword by Ken Blanchard

I have no doubt that the ideas you have just read will make a difference in the way you lead. But I have an important question: Are you motivated to lead? Ha! I know that is a silly question, so let me ask, *Why* are you motivated to lead?

I am thoroughly convinced that great leadership comes from the heart—a servant leader's heart. Servant leadership is impossible when you lead with a suboptimal motivational outlook.

If you lead from the disinterested motivational outlook, you are not leading anyone to anywhere meaningful. If you lead from the external motivational outlook, focused on building organizational assets or your own legacy, you are keeping your eye on the scoreboard and missing the most important part of the game that helps guarantee *sustainable* success—helping your people flourish. If you lead with an imposed motivational outlook, your misery becomes your people's misery, which becomes your customer's misery.

Your optimal motivational outlook, on the other hand, generates a positive ripple effect as long as you don't allow your own enthusiasm to impose your ideas and values on people. Discuss what you have learned and hope to do differently. If you are a situational leader, have alignment conversations where you and your direct reports agree on

157

their goal. Then facilitate motivational outlook conversations asking the pivotal question, *Why* are you motivated to achieve this goal? As you have discovered, individuals with a suboptimal motivational outlook while pursuing their goal will have a very different experience than those with an optimal motivational outlook. Equipped with your understanding of people's motivational outlook, you can provide the appropriate direction and support for them to attain and maintain high-quality competence and commitment.

Servant leaders, and the best situational leaders, are optimally motivated. They find meaning by aligning their leadership decisions and actions to developed values. They integrate their work with a noble purpose. They find inherent joy in positively influencing people's lives and contributing to society. You make a difference as a leader. What kind of difference will you make? If you put the ideas from this book into action, you will have a better chance of being a servant leader rather than a self-serving one.

Amazon's Hall of Fame recently inducted Ken Blanchard as one of the top twenty-five best-selling authors of all time. He and Susan have coauthored three books together.[1]

• Epilogue: Masters of Motivation

Think about the best boss you ever had. Who comes to mind? Chances are, whoever comes into your mind had something in common with the leaders profiled in this section: a mindful approach to leadership based on highly developed values and a noble purpose. As you will discover, some of the masters profiled lead instinctively using the ideas in this book, others purposely implemented the ideas, and two of the masters fathered the science at the core of the ideas. Over fifteen years I have witnessed these Masters of Motivation creating workplaces where people flourish and—as a result, seen their customers and metrics flourish as well.

I imagine a decade from now seeing a young, emerging leader reading the fifth edition of this book. My dream is that when that young leader answers the question of who is the best boss he or she ever had, the person who comes to mind will be you. I hope that by applying the ideas outlined in this book, you will become someone's Master of Motivation.

Phil Jackson
Uncommon Methods, Uncommon Results

Phil Jackson is the president of the New York Knicks basketball organization. When he stepped out of his self-induced coaching retirement into the presidency of the Knicks in a five-year, $60 million deal, many in the media described it as a money and power grab. After all, what else would uproot the sixty-eight-year-old from his family and fiancée on the West Coast to the hustle and bustle of New York at this point in his life?

A deeper understanding of Phil's approach to life and work reveals different reasons for his decision than what's been reported. As the most-winning coach in National Basketball Association (NBA) history, Phil knows how to satisfy psychological needs—his own and those of the players he has coached. Now he has the opportunity to shape and hone an entire organization through his values and sensibility. He will have the authority to make key decisions (autonomy). He will offer well-developed values to help infuse the Knicks with a deeper sense of purpose and meaning and tap into his vast network to attract talent (relatedness). He will use the insight from almost fifty years of playing and coaching in the NBA to build a just and winning organization (competence).

Phil has been called some interesting names in his storied career—several he'd probably rather forget, some he has outlived, and a few he doesn't mind. He picked up one of his famous nicknames, the Zen Master, from his use of meditation and other rituals in the locker room. He used what many consider unconventional ways to teach his players self-regulation through mindfulness. It was important for these players, so tempted by the pressures of big paychecks, fame, and power, to move beyond external motivators. As Phil would say, he wanted them to wake up, if only for a moment, to see the unseen, hear the unheard, and access their abundant inner resources that are instrumental for a higher-quality experience.

Whatever you call Phil, there are impressive links between his approach to leadership and the science of motivation described in this book. It should be noted that Phil is skeptical of many books on leadership. In his experience, the so-called universal principles in most leadership textbooks rarely hold up. He believes that to shift a culture from one stage to the next, you need to find the levers that are appropriate for that particular stage in the group's development. The same is true with motivation. You cannot hope to motivate people in meaningful ways if you don't understand the levers that influence the way people are motivated.

Over Phil's years of experience, it became clear to him that the levers for motivation were different than many coaches assumed. In his book *Eleven Rings*, he reveals there are two kinds of coaches: those who lead teams to victory and those who *drive* them. After being coached by and coaching with ego-driven coaches who think driving people to excellence works, Phil seems to have opted for the former approach.[1] The antithesis of driving for results is creating a workplace where people don't have to use their precious energy to cope with external pressures that inhibit their inner resources.

Through his creative exploration of what truly and deeply motivates people, Phil discovered refreshing alternatives to driving people to success. His tactics may have seemed foreign to many of his players, but they bought in. Now the science of motivation sheds light on *why* his approach worked to help win six championships in Chicago and five in Los Angeles. The big-stakes world of professional sports that Phil works in is prone to distractions that can take people away from what's really important in work and life. He has always been more interested in having players focus on the pass that leads to the score.

Phil Jackson's success reminds us why it is important to keep our focus on what's really important in our work as leaders. As Phil says, "That kind of awareness takes time to develop, but once you've mastered it, the invisible becomes visible and the game unfolds like a story before your eyes."[2]

Colleen Barrett
ARC Takes Flight

Colleen Barrett is president emeritus of Southwest Airlines. *President emeritus* is an honorary title bestowed as recognition for exemplary service. But Colleen is a woman of action, so she still goes to work daily at Southwest's headquarters in Dallas—not because she has official responsibilities or is being held accountable for results but because she is intent on sustaining a company culture she helped craft over forty years ago.

If you have flown Southwest Airlines, you know that culture is front and center—from the uniforms worn by employees to the flight attendants' pretakeoff announcements. On a recent flight, our flight attendant came on the PA system with this question: "Who dropped this wallet?" We all looked up to see if it was our wallet. Then he said, "Great, now that I have everyone's attention, please check to see that your seatbelts are securely fastened." Passengers on the entire plane broke into laughter and paid attention to the rest of the safety announcement.

That sense of humor is standard operating procedure for Southwest, but it didn't come easily. It took the leadership of Colleen and her staff, working with and convincing the FAA and consumer groups that not only were their flight attendants covering all the safety regulations required by law but that people were actually listening to them. When told that Southwest's uniforms were too casual, Colleen made the argument for them by asking, "In an emergency, would you rather have someone in comfortable slacks and tennis shoes or high heels and nylons?"

Colleen's tenure at Southwest meant fighting bureaucracy every single day. What she was really fighting for was her people's sense of autonomy. As long as her people were able to meet safety regulations, she fought for their creative license. She never believed that people should leave their personalities in their cars on the way to work, put on a uniform, and then walk, talk, and quack like every other duck. "I explained to people that we hired you for you. We hire different people for different reasons. Play off your strengths. I think Southwest has benefited from the diversity of individuals being themselves and then coming together as a team."

The power of ARC is in full effect at Southwest. The autonomy that Colleen fought to provide for people demonstrated a trust in their competence for decision making and doing their jobs effectively. By fighting for their autonomy and trusting in their competence, she helped people experience a sense of relatedness.

Colleen goes so far as to call it love. She knows that *love* is not a word often used in corporate America, but she insists the love is real at Southwest Airlines. As president, she demonstrates her love through her direct honesty. There is nothing soft about Colleen, but she loves people enough to tell them the truth when their performance isn't meeting expectations or they disappointed a customer. She has even fired customers. For example, acknowledging that Southwest's best efforts and good intentions couldn't satisfy a particular woman, Colleen wished her well as she flew with a competitor.

Colleen is adamant when she says, "Leaders need to demonstrate they care by devoting more time to interpersonal interactions with their people. I took my leadership role seriously, and granted, there was little time for sleep. But I felt the time I invested in communicating to, celebrating with, and acknowledging thousands of employees through personal notes, phone calls, and meetings was time well invested."

During her retirement, Colleen still demonstrates love through her investment of time—actively embracing employees, retirees, customers, and business partners on a daily basis. The success of Southwest Airlines is certainly proof that the culture of autonomy, relatedness, and competence that Colleen Barrett helped establish worked then and continues to have wings today.

Mike Easley
CEO Drills Deep

Mike Easley is CEO of Powder River Energy Corporation (PREcorp) in Gillette, Wyoming. Talk about the Wild West. PREcorp is a cooperative that brings energy to rural areas too remote for a public utility company to bother. In the past couple of years, Mike and his leadership team instituted a strategic execution model that is yielding 20 percent value added to his cooperative's members. Ask Mike about how he's generating such success in this rugged world of energy, power, and cowboys who happen to be linemen, and you might be surprised by what you hear.

Mike reached a turning point in his career in 2011 when he decided to leave PREcorp and embark on a job search. When his dream job fell through, he fell into a funk. During this time, he was asked to provide the music for a religious service at a local nursing home, something he'd done in the past. That particular evening, the minister didn't make it. Mike found himself conducting the service, leading prayers, and playing his guitar. It was a life-changing moment. Mike says he experienced a meaningful connection with each individual in the service and his music. He felt a deep sense of joy from contributing to the welfare of others.

Mike was an early adopter of the ideas in this book. His entire leadership team attended beta tests in the early days of the development of the Optimal Motivation workshop. That night in the nursing home, Mike recognized how hungry he had been for a sense of relatedness. He made visiting the nursing home a weekly ritual. He started opening himself up and it made everything better—his music, writing, singing, compassion, and empathy for others. He started to challenge his introverted nature and found himself conversing more freely. It dawned on him that he was one Mike, not a group of compartmentalized Mikes—one guy at home, another at work, and another when playing music to senior citizens. He was eager to experience relatedness. He wanted the joy he felt at the nursing home in other parts of his life.

He discovered that it was a quest for relatedness that had sent him job searching. As CEO of PREcorp, he had autonomy. With all his years of experience, he had competence. He didn't need a new job; he needed a sense of relatedness at PREcorp.

Mike turned his energy back to the organization he had been so ready to leave. He implemented a visioning process. He involved PREcorp employees in a video talking about the role Powder River Energy has played in their lives and in the community. He worked with the board to change his role, passing most of his operational duties to a new COO so he could focus on building a new culture. Mike wanted others to experience relatedness at work.

With PREcorp's standout results, Mike's team is training one hundred other energy co-ops throughout the United States on PREcorp's new strategic execution system. He is dedicated to making the entire industry stronger. Mike continues to reflect on his personal turnaround: "I never want to settle. Yet I want to be at peace and continue to grow in a positive way. I think leaders need to develop the skills they hope their employees and teammates will have. I don't know how else you can be a leader worth following. But if you want to be a leader worth following, you need to be able to lead yourself first. I don't want to look over my shoulder at the end of my career and see carnage left behind.

"Motivating people doesn't work—a state of mind needs to be invited. I want to look ahead and see the legacy of a gentler, kinder, nicer me, supporting others in their success. If I am going to be a servant leader, I need to carry the love I found in the nursing home with all the Mikes—to be an integrated human being across every spectrum of my life."

Billy Yamaguchi
Leading with Style

Billy Yamaguchi is co-owner of Yamaguchi Salons. I enjoyed his book, *Feng Shui Beauty*,[3] but I wondered what a celebrity stylist who worked on the likes of Jennifer Aniston could say as a guest speaker to the young women at our Angel Faces Retreat. These were girls who had been traumatized and disfigured in tragic burn accidents. A focus on Hollywood's idea of beauty was the exact opposite of the ideal of inner beauty we hoped to instill in the girls.

As he spent the afternoon working his magic with the girls, Billy won us all over, telling them, "It's really important for you to own who you are because there are a lot of people who don't recognize the beauty within them." He emphasized connecting with who they are on the inside and reflecting that on the outside. He was a revelation. Billy's profound joy in serving his clients was obvious—whether they're celebrities or terribly scarred young women. Billy proved to be a master of motivation when it came to bringing out the inner beauty of his clients.

But he confessed he felt less confident when it came to the motivation of his salon staff. Although one of his salons was named one of California's top five salons and one of the twenty-five best reasons to visit California, Billy still struggled to understand a stylist who wasn't enthusiastic about building her own clientele or taking advantage of the opportunities provided for her to grow, learn, and get better. It was perplexing to him if a stylist failed to mirror his enthusiasm and work ethic.

As many successful entrepreneurs and leaders do, Billy assumed that his staff would be motivated in the same way he is—and for the same reasons. He tried to infuse his values and sense of purpose in others. But when it didn't work as he hoped, he began exploring alternatives to traditional ways of "motivating."

Then he discovered why motivating people doesn't work. People are motivated by their own values and purpose, not *his* values and *his* sense of purpose. They aren't motivated by external rewards or fear of losing their job. He and his management team took a different course of action. Ironically, Billy began practicing with his staff what he was so masterful in doing for his clients—bringing out the best within them and expressing it on the outside. Billy explains, "We invested the time to work with our staff, helping them develop their own workplace values and purpose. Now when we make requests, such as attending a training session, trying a new styling technique, or helping build the business, we also facilitate motivational outlook conversations to help them understand if and how these requests are linked to their own values and purpose. We facilitate their shift between a suboptimal and an optimal motivational outlook. We help them get in touch with why they come to work every day.

"Our staff is more satisfied with their work, and our clients can feel the difference. The added bonus is the renewed energy that my management staff and I feel. I always loved caring for my clients. Now I get as much joy from bringing out the best in my staff as I do my clients."

Garry Ridge
A Special Formula for Success

Garry Ridge is the president and CEO of the WD-40 Company. Ask Garry how the company is doing, and off the top of his head he showers you with employee engagement scores of 93.8 percent—three times the national average. Retention rates are equally high. It has a market cap that's grown from $200 million to $1.2 billion and has exceeded the performance of the Russell 2000 and S&P by a long shot over the last ten years. The brand is stronger than ever.

Ask Garry how he and the company have achieved such outstanding results, and he responds as smoothly as WD-40 Company's industrial lubricant. He is convinced their success is built on a culture of belonging. He is quick to point out that belonging is not all "kumbaya." Belonging, he explains, is a balance between being tough-minded and being tenderhearted. This place in between is where people feel safe and able to do their best work.

The number one answer (98 percent of the responses) from WD-40 Company's 2012 employee engagement survey is, "At WD-40 Company, I am treated with respect and dignity." But how do Garry and his leaders demonstrate respect for others? WD-40's formula for success may be a secret, but Garry's secret for business success isn't. He cites three important practices.

"The first is taking time. The one thing a leader has to give that they can never take back is time. It sends a powerful message to people when you say, 'I want to spend time with you because I care about you; I mean you no harm.' There is a connection between care and candor. I care enough about you to be honest about how you can grow. I care enough about you to help you be the next version of your best self.

"The second practice is helping people move from fear to freedom. We have eliminated one of people's greatest fears—the fear of failure. People do not fail at WD-40 Company, they have learning moments—a positive or negative outcome of any situation that needs to be openly and freely shared among the tribe. We celebrate learning moments.

"The third practice is to help people appreciate the value of values. Rather than imposing values on people, we understand the power of people developing their own values using the company's values as a model. Values conversations are frequent. Managers share their leadership point of view, describing how their own values influence their decisions, actions, and approach to leadership. When people realize that acting from the company's values feels good, they tend to develop their own values aligned with ours."

Garry's approach to business promotes a workplace that makes it easier for people to self-regulate. People aren't expending emotional labor on low-quality self-regulation just to satisfy their psychological needs. Either by happy accident or by intelligent design, Garry has tapped into the interconnected power of ARC. People exercise autonomy within clearly defined and fair expectations and boundaries. People feel relatedness through a culture of belonging. People recognize their ever-growing competence by focusing on learning moments that encourage them to try something new, ask for help, and learn from their experiences.

Garry knows, "There's no such thing as a single motivation. People choose their own motivation. A leader's job is to create an environment that makes it easier for people to choose optimal motivation. It takes dedication to create that safe playing field where people can move from fear to freedom, protected by values and inspired by vision. Our real job is to help all our people be the next version of their best self. It is time well invested."

Dr. Beth Scalone
Practicing Healthy Leadership

Dr. Beth Scalone is owner of North County Water and Sports Therapy Center. I could applaud her motivation skills solely based on her work with my husband and me as longtime clients. Oh, the stories she could tell. But the real story that needs sharing is Beth's leadership as a sole proprietor of a small business.

I recommended Beth to a colleague suffering with muscle deterioration from exposure to Agent Orange while he was serving in the Vietnam War. Because of scheduling conflicts, Beth assigned Dick to one of her employees,

Kathleen. Several weeks later, Dick called me with profuse thanks, declaring, "Kathleen has changed my life! I have been in and out of physical therapy for years, but this is the first time it has made a difference. I could barely walk when I came in; now I have almost full use of my right leg. It feels like a miracle."

Another miracle is how Beth's employees are optimally motivated to emulate and demonstrate her values of quality care and excellence. Beth may have been named Aquatic Therapy Professional of the year in 2012, but she confesses there's a big difference between being a good therapist and being a good leader of other therapists.

Beth says, "I have learned how to work with my clients —to guide them through their fears and anger after tragic accidents, break through cultural barriers, communicate with different personality types, and build trust in a medical environment that can be downright maddening. I demonstrate patience with my patients, but I am not prone to mollycoddling my employees. As a manager, my attitude is 'Like it, lump it, and get on with it.'"

So how has this no-nonsense leader developed a staff of long-tenured, dedicated employees who create raving fans?

- *Beth will tell you she hires them*—That is part of it. Beth has such a clear set of values, sense of purpose, and strong work ethic that applicants know when they fit in—or don't. Those who become part of the family feel a sense of relatedness from the very beginning.

- *Beth's employees will tell you that she instills respect*— How? Ryann, a physical therapist, explains, "Beth is the best at what she does. She is busy and works long hours. Still, she notices, she pays attention to what I do—not as a way to monitor or micromanage me but to provide information that makes me a better therapist and bring better care to my clients. She doesn't do a lot of praising—I can tell when I have done a good job because she tells me how she just learned something from watching me or comments on the improvement she noticed in my client. You know that movie about the little pig, *Babe*, who set out to win over the other barnyard animals and the farmer? I feel like Beth is like Farmer Hoggett standing beside me saying, 'That'll do, pig.' It's a quiet and powerful acknowledgment that I am good at what I do."

I find it intriguing that leaders who help employees respect their own competence earn the respect of their employees.

- *Beth understands that power generates more power when it is given away*—All the physical therapists on Beth's staff are empowered to do what it takes to satisfy the needs of clients, meet the demands of insurance companies, and keep the clinic humming. She encourages her staff to give *her* feedback when her behavior is less than desirable as a boss. She and her office manager even agreed on a code word to use if Beth's actions are undermining autonomy, relatedness, or competence.

Beth admits, "At the end of the day, it's humbling to be an owner and realize that when you give people the freedom to do good work, they will. They make me look good!"

Matt Manion
Good Leader, Good Shepherd

Matt Manion is president and CEO of the Catholic Leadership Institute (CLI). When Matt talks about CLI, it is difficult not to be infused with his sense of purpose and his spirit. CLI has a mission to help strengthen priests' identity, ministry, and fraternity through a unique integrated leadership curriculum—the only one of its kind serving the United States Church.

CLI was an early adopter of the Spectrum of Motivation model. According to Matt, the reason more than one-third of his organization's twenty-two-month learning experience is devoted to self leadership and personal development is that priests cannot give what they don't have. "Priests need to be an instrument of the gospel. If they are broken, if they cannot self-regulate, if they are not mindful of their own emotions and needs, they are ill-equipped to meet the needs of others."

Matt explains that priests are faced with the challenges of a diminishing number of clergy and complex circumstances such as the clustering of parishes that can triple a priest's responsibilities. "Not only are priests dealing with the complexities of creating and building an authentic, vibrant Catholic community, but they are struggling with higher expectations than employees might have for leaders outside the church. The pressures and demands of their role often make it more difficult for the priests to represent the spiritual practices that define why they became priests in the first place. They often feel they are letting everyone down, including themselves."

Learning to shift their motivational outlook is a big part of the priests' learning experience. It's easy to sabotage their own psychological needs in the midst of so many demands. Sometimes they forget they have autonomy, even though the church structure promotes it. Sometimes they need a reminder of their purpose, their deep relationship with parishioners, and their intimate connection with Christ. The challenges of governance have undermined their sense of competence. However, when they graduate from the Good Leaders, Good Shepherds program, they have gained skills to govern effectively and a greater sense of competence.

From the very beginning of their twenty-two-month learning journey, priests work on the mechanisms to help shift their motivational outlook. They practice the MVPs of self-regulation, starting with mindfulness—an awareness of their feelings and emotions as they run what equates to a midsize business. They challenge potentially programmed values and take the time to reflect on their developed values. They craft role-related purpose statements. They set meaningful goals aligned with parish goals and the expectations of the church and their bishop. They discover their personality types, natural patterns of behavior, and the reasons that some activities tend to zap more energy than others.

Through Good Leaders, Good Shepherds, over two thousand priests are learning to shift from suboptimal to optimal motivational outlooks. Their shift minimizes the frustration and energy spent on administrative roles and maximizes the joy and time spent on the pastoral duties for which they were uniquely ordained. Matt explains that priests come to realize that it is important not to be caught up in simply getting stuff done but to question why they're doing it. "Priests find themselves renewed. Ultimately, through their mindfulness, values, and purpose shaped by faith, they realize they need to build the kingdom here."

Dr. Margie Blanchard
Framing Good Intentions

Margie Blanchard is cofounder of the Ken Blanchard Companies. Years ago, as president of the company, Margie became a fierce advocate of regular and formalized one-on-one meetings between managers and their employees as a way to improve relationships and foster the company's flagship programs, Situational Leadership II and Situational Self Leadership. Margie sheepishly explains what it took to make one-on-one meetings an integral part of the organization's culture: "We had to pay managers to do them. We paid each manager $200 per direct report for conducting biweekly one-on-one meetings. It's not something I am proud to admit, but I am proud that today these conversations are a centerpiece of our culture because people recognize their value."

Let me be quick to point out that Margie's approach worked not because she was paying people but because she framed her proposal in a way that enabled people to see it through an optimal motivational outlook. She explained to people: "We believe this practice is so vital to building successful relationships, honoring our values, and being a role model to our clients that I am willing to pay you to do it for one year. After this year, I trust that the value of the practice will speak for itself." As a witness from the beginning, I can attest that this is exactly what happened.

Margie recommends that if you feel the need to sweeten the pot to get people to try what's good for them, be careful how you position the proposal.

- Focus on the behavior you want to see.

- Demonstrate that you are empathetic about how individual concerns might be impacted.

- Perhaps most importantly, remind people that the reward is not a carrot to entice their compliance but a reflection of how strongly you believe in the benefit of the behavior.

Do not offer money as a reward but rather as a statement of how important the behavior, goal, or activity is to them and the organization.

Margie adds, "Today, instead of rewarding people to do what the organization needs done, we are more likely to call on managers to facilitate motivational outlook conversations. A robust outlook conversation is a healthy alternative to bribing people with carrots."

Dr. Scott Rigby, Dr. Richard Ryan, and Dr. Edward Deci
Playing with Purpose

Dr. Scott Rigby, Dr. Richard Ryan, and Dr. Edward Deci are cofounders of Immersyve. They are dedicated to the study and application of motivation science to the worlds of gaming, education, organizational behavior, and health care.

Ed and Rich, the founders of Self-Determination Theory, are perhaps the most prominent motivation researchers in the world. So why are they involved in gaming—and how does it relate to leadership?

For starters, if you don't play some type of online, interactive game, you are in the minority. In the United States, games generate almost twice the revenue of movies.[4] The biggest-selling video game, World of Warcraft, has generated over $10 billion compared to the number one movie of all time, *Avatar*, at less than $3 billion. Explains Rich, "Games have an incredible motivational pull. The better we understand the deeper psychology behind the palpable love people have for video games, the more we can harness that energy to enhance education, training, and the development of social and leadership skills."

An area of special interest for leaders is the growing phenomenon of "gamification." Not surprisingly, gamification has gained popularity in sales divisions that traditionally use external incentives to promote sales, believing that most salespeople are motivated by money, trips, and winning. But ironically, gamification is being embraced by human resource departments that have the best intentions of improving their employees' health and well-being. Indeed, gaming is being endorsed more broadly by organizations for facilitating effective performance. But the experts at Immersyve warn against implementing gamification strategies without the insight of motivation science, especially ideas such as those presented in this book based on self-determination theory.

When it comes to gamification, Scott points out, "Many companies rush too quickly to gamification, making the mistake of confusing the *tactic* of game mechanics as the *goal*. They turn internal websites for sales or human resources into games or contests that can often lead to ill-advised decisions to wrap glitzy badges and rewards around experiences. Those tactics not only don't *sustain* motivation or build value but can actually hurt the relationship with employees because it communicates that the value lies in the badges and points, rather than the substance of your business or the health of your employees."

Scott, Rich, and Ed offer two key pieces of advice if you are considering games and contests to "motivate" employees:

- *Don't begin with the goal to create a gamelike approach—* Begin with the intent to create a vehicle where people can be optimally motivated and sustain engagement. Scott explains, "Thoughtful application of game design can facilitate an authentic satisfaction of people's psychological needs for autonomy, relatedness, and competence. Understanding the nature of human motivation is essential for communicating to employees that your organization and its offerings are where the value lies— not the badges and confetti sprinkled on top."

- *Think about rewards versus motivation—*The two concepts are very different and can even be antagonistic. Research confirms that games based on reinforcing performance through rewards rather than recognizing and supporting intrinsic motivators do not yield enjoyment and immersion (which increase comprehension and competence), the likelihood a person will play next week (indicating sustained engagement and autonomy), and a preference to play more games by a particular developer (reflecting loyalty and relatedness).[5]

According to Ed, who did the first studies of monetary rewards and intrinsic motivation, "Giving rewards as reinforcements undermines short-term learning and long-term engagement in games—and goals in the workplace. However, people will find activities intrinsically *rewarding* and more deeply satisfying when their autonomy, relatedness, and competence are respected, encouraged, and supported by elements of a game—and by their managers at work."

• Frequently Asked Questions

1. Is there ever a time when rewards are appropriate?

Rewards may not be appropriate, but you might decide they are necessary. For example, the FAA is offering a $10,000 reward to anyone reporting a person pointing lasers at airplanes in flight. The danger posed to pilots, passengers, and people on the ground was too great to ignore. It's a sad commentary that you would sell out a friend for $10,000. It is even sadder to think that if you knew people were threatening lives using a laser, you wouldn't either do whatever it took to stop them yourself or voluntarily turn them in because it's the right thing to do. Rewards are necessary if people don't have the self-regulation necessary to do the right thing through mindfulness, developed values, or a noble purpose.

2. I need people to achieve goals and meet deadlines. How do I make expectations clear without putting people into an imposed motivational outlook?

As a leader, you are responsible for making sure that people achieve the organization's goals. But you have the ability to frame those goals—or help people reframe them—so goals are more meaningful and relevant to individuals.

We will never be free of delegated goals and deadlines. However, leaders can present deadlines as necessary and helpful data. Leaders can encourage individuals to consider deadlines as valuable information for allocating time effectively, making thoughtful choices, and determining what a priority is—or is not.

3. Why do you refer to suboptimal and optimal motivational outlooks instead of extrinsic and intrinsic motivation?

The extrinsic-intrinsic model has served to prove how wrong traditional approaches to motivation have been. However, the simplistic duality renders it difficult to apply. Realistically, what percentage of a person's workday can be attributed to purely intrinsic activities? The latest research indicates that some forms of extrinsic motivation provide the same or maybe even higher-quality benefits as intrinsic motivation. These are represented in the Spectrum of Motivation model by the aligned and integrated motivational outlooks. Choosing to shift to an optimal motivational outlook based on developed values, meaningful goals, and a sense of purpose enables people to take advantage of the benefits of intrinsic motivation, even if they are not purely intrinsically motivated.

4. Are there clues in people's language about their motivational outlook?

Phrases or thoughts that tend to reflect suboptimal motivational outlooks include the following:

I have to
I must
I should
I am required to
It is necessary
Because it is my duty to
I am getting paid to do this
I'll be sorry if I don't do this
I don't want to let you down
I have to follow the rules
I want to make you proud
I may be afraid of disappointing you or myself
It's all about the results
I owe it to you

Phrases or thoughts that tend to reflect an optimal motivational outlook include the following:
I get to
I have decided to
I am lucky to
I elect to
I have selected to
I ought to
I am able to
I have the pleasure of
It is a privilege to act on my values
It is personal and I value the relationship
I will grow and learn as a result of doing this
This is what I choose to do
I enjoy this
I have a rationale for this

I choose to follow the rules

I understand the purpose behind what I do

I experienced the joy of contributing to something greater
than myself

5. The younger generation's values drive me crazy. They'd rather be online with their friends than work because their parents will pay their bills. How can I motivate this generation?

If you don't know how to motivate the younger generation, don't despair. Remember, motivating people doesn't
work—no matter what the generation. People born within
the same period tend to assume the same programmed values as their peers.[1] As a leader, your role is to help them
explore programmed values and *develop meaningful values* that are freely chosen from alternatives with an understanding of the consequences of the alternatives, prized
and cherished, and acted upon over time.[2] Taking the time
to help the younger generation consciously develop their
values facilitates their shift to an optimal motivational outlook by helping them link their situation to those values
and sense of purpose.

6. Why do you say contests don't work? People seem to respond to them and contests can grab people's attention to something they might not have had an initial interest in exploring.

If you are using a contest to "motivate" people, ask yourself why. If it is to create a fun experience, like a carnival,
then fine. However, if you're running a contest to attract
attention to an important message or encourage certain

behaviors, contests are risky. They distract people from your primary message, shifting the focus to the contest or prize.[3] Do you need people to continue paying attention or behaving in a certain way after the contest is over? If so, spend the time and energy to provide a values-based rationale for their doing what you are asking of them. Consider how people's psychological needs for autonomy, relatedness, and competence will be better satisfied by doing what you're asking them to do. Contests are easy and fast and may get an immediate reaction. To avoid creating a game or contest that is motivation junk food, refer to the book *Glued to Games* by Scott Rigby and Richard Ryan.[4]

7. Why isn't competition a good thing? Great athletes, chefs, and salespeople seem to thrive on competition. Can't it bring out the best in people?

Scratch beneath the surface of superstars in any field and you will find that their primary reason for competing has more to do with their choice to dedicate time and effort to a particular endeavor (autonomy); a sense of purpose, camaraderie, and service (relatedness); a quest for excellence (competence); or the pure enjoyment for doing what they have chosen to do. They may say winning is everything, but what they really mean is that winning provides data. Winning and losing present a scoreboard of information they use to make sounder choices, determine how to continue growing and learning, and find ways for better serving their customers, teammates, or fans. Even non-superstars will benefit from understanding that it is not being a competitor that makes a difference—it's the reason you compete that makes a difference.

• Notes

Introduction

1. Kleinginna and Kleinginna, "Categorized List."
2. Deci et al., "Benefits of Giving Autonomy Support."
3. Baard, "Intrinsic Need Satisfaction"; Deci and Ryan, *Handbook of Self-Determination Research*; Gagne and Deci, "Self-Determination Theory"; and Deci and Ryan, "Facilitating Optimal Motivation."
4. Kohn, *Punished by Rewards*.
5. Murayama et al., "Undermining Effect of Monetary Reward"; and Kerr, Feltz, and Irwin, "To Pay or Not to Pay?"
6. Ryan, "Self-Determination Theory"; Deci and Ryan, *Handbook of Self-Determination Research*; Deci and Ryan, "Facilitating Optimal Motivation"; and Pink, *Drive*.

Chapter 1

1. "Beane Happy to Run A's through 2008."
2. Zigarmi et al., "Employee Work Passion Model."
3. Hagger, Chatzisarantis, and Harris, "Psychological Need Satisfaction."
4. Zigarmi et al., "Beyond Engagement."
5. Meyer and Gagne, "Employee Engagement."
6. Zigarmi and Nimon. "A Cognitive Approach"; and Hagger, Chatzisarantis, and Harris "Psychological Need Satisfaction."
7. Nimon and Zigarmi, "Work Cognition Inventory."
8. Definition by Susan Fowler, David Facer, and Drea Zigarmi.
9. Spectrum of Motivation model by Susan Fowler, David Facer, and Drea Zigarmi.

10. Moller et al., "Financial Motivation Undermines Maintenance."
11. Ibid.; Kennedy, "Firms Bet Money Will Prod Employees."
12. Kovach, "Why Motivational Theories Don't Work."
13. Deci and Ryan, *Handbook of Self-Determination Research*; Deci and Ryan, "Facilitating Optimal Motivation"; Kasser, *High Price of Materialism*; Gagne and Deci, "Self-Determination Theory"; Murayama et al., "Undermining Effect of Monetary Reward"; and Kerr, Feltz, and Irwin, "To Pay or Not to Pay?"
14. Ibid.

Chapter 2

1. This is a great example of the intersection between the Situational Leadership II model and the Spectrum of Motivation model. Oftentimes, an individual's need for autonomy will cloud the diagnosis of his development level. According to SLII, he is at the D1 level of development with low competence and high commitment on a goal, task, or skill, but his need to "do it for himself" despite lacking the competence, has him misdiagnosing himself at the D4 level of development with high competence and high commitment.
2. Patall, Cooper, and Robinson, "Effects of Choice"; and Radel et al., "Restoration Process of Autonomy."
3. Deci et al., "Need Satisfaction, Motivation and Well-Being"; and Gagne and Deci, "Self-Determination Theory."
4. Frankl, *Man's Search for Meaning*.
5. Berinato, "Shut Up Already."
6. Irwin, Feltz, and Kerr, "Silence Is Golden"; and Kerr, Feltz, and Irwin, "To Pay or Not to Pay?"
7. Ibid. Also, interview with Dr. Irwin, November 2013.
8. Fehr and Renninger, "Samaritan Paradox."
9. Christakis and Fowler, *Connected*.
10. Tay and Diener, "Needs and Subjective Well-Being"; and Milyavskaya et al., "Balance across Contexts."

Chapter 3

1. Ryan and Deci, "Ego Depletion to Vitality"; and Deci and Ryan, "Facilitating Optimal Motivation."
2. Spectrum of Motivation model by Susan Fowler, David Facer, and Drea Zigarmi.
3. Definition by Susan Fowler, David Facer, and Drea Zigarmi.
4. Ayduk et al., "Regulating the Interpersonal Self"; and Vohs and Baumeister, *Handbook of Self-Regulation*.
5. Mischel, Ebbesen, and Zeiss, "Cognitive and Attentional Mechanisms"; Mischel, Shoda, and Rodriguez, "Delay of Gratification"; and Schlam et al., "Preschoolers' Delay of Gratification."
6. Kidd, Palmeri, and Aslin, "Rational Snacking."
7. Gillet et al., "Impact of Organizational Factors."
8. Brown and Ryan, "Benefits of Being Present"; Brown, Ryan, and Creswell, "Mindfulness"; Brown and Holt, "Experiential Processing"; Jenkins and Tapper, "Resisting Chocolate Temptation"; and Ryback, "Neurology of Mindfulness."
9. Hitlin and Piliavin, "Values."
10. Garfield, *Peak Performers*.

Chapter 4

1. Ryan, Bernstein, and Brown, "Weekends, Work, and Well-Being."
2. Gagne et al., "Temporal Analysis"; and Deci and Ryan, "Facilitating Optimal Motivation."
3. Csikszentmihalyi, *Flow*.
4. Zigarmi and Nimon, "A Cognitive Approach"; and Kotsou, Mikolajczak, and Nelis, "Emotional Plasticity."
5. Page and Vella-Brodrick, "Employee Well-Being"; Deci and Ryan, *Handbook of Self-Determination Research*; and Edmonds and Zigarmi, L., *#Positivity at Work Tweet Book*.
6. Reeve, *Understanding Motivation and Emotion*.
7. The following are three resources for more specific statistics and research: *The Economics of Wellbeing* by Tom Rath

and Jim Harter (New York: Gallup Press, 2010), *Positive Intelligence* by Shawn Achor (*Harvard Business Review*, January/February 2012), and the Self-Determination Theory website at http://www.selfdeterminationtheory.org.

Chapter 5

1. Rock, *Your Brain at Work*. Rock's SCARF model includes status as a basic need for motivation. Indeed, it is, but for suboptimal motivation. Status undermines relatedness. Ryan and Deci, "From Ego Depletion to Vitality."
2. Ryan and Connell, "Perceived Locus of Causality and Internalization."
3. Zigarmi and Roberts, "Leader Values as Predictors."
4. Executive coaches often guard against asking the question why. I agree that when used to discuss past behavior or future intentions in a problem-solving mode, the question could lead to a defensive reaction. An outlook conversation is not about problem solving or determining behavior but digging deeper to understand how psychological needs are being satisfied or thwarted. Ironically, often this basic understanding leads to solving problems and developing action plans for the future—but that is not the original intention.
5. Smith and Clurman, *Generation Ageless*.

Chapter 6

1. Kovach, "Why Motivational Theories Don't Work"; and Facer et al. "Motivation Beliefs Inventory."
2. Facer et al., "Motivation Beliefs Inventory."
3. Optimal Motivation by Susan Fowler, David Facer, and Drea Zigarmi.
4. Zigarmi et al., *Leadership-Profit Chain*.
5. Optimal Motivation by Susan Fowler, David Facer, and Drea Zigarmi.
6. Interview with Dr. Drea Zigarm, February 2014.
7. Ibid.

8. Optimal Motivation by Susan Fowler, David Facer, and Drea Zigarmi.

9. Sheldon et al. "Effects of Goal Contents and Motives."

10. Ibid.

11. Optimal Motivation by Susan Fowler, David Facer, and Drea Zigarmi.

12. Ibid.

Chapter 7
1. Dweck, *Mindset*.

Afterword
1. Blanchard and Fowler, *Empowerment*; Blanchard, Fowler, and Hawkins, *Self Leadership and the One Minute Manager*; and Blanchard, et al., *Leading at a Higher Level*.

Epilogue
1. Jackson, *Sacred Hoops.*

2. Jackson and Delehanty, *Eleven Rings*, 101.

3. Yamaguchi, *Feng Shui Beauty.*

4. In the United States, gaming generated $17.02 billion in 2011, according to the NPD Group, while movie sales in the United States generated $9.42 billion according to The-Numbers .com. Bronkhorst, "Games vs. Movies."

5. Rigby and Ryan, *Glued to Games.*

Frequently Asked Questions
1. Howe and Strauss, *Generations.*

2. Zigarmi, Fowler, and Lyles, *Achieve Leadership Genius.*

3. Rigby and Ryan, *Glued to Games.*

4. Ibid.

Resources
1. Zigarmi et al., *The Leader Within.*

• Bibliography

Ayduk, O. N., R. Mendoza-Denton, W. Mischel, G. Downey, P. K. Peake, and M. L. Rodriguez. "Regulating the Interpersonal Self: Strategic Self-Regulation for Coping with Rejection Sensitivity." *Journal of Personality and Social Psychology* 79, no. 5 (2000): 776–792.

Baard, Paul P. "Intrinsic Need Satisfaction in Organizations: A Motivational Basis of Success in for-Profit and Not-for-Profit Settings." In *Handbook of Self-Determination Research*, edited by Edward L. Deci and Richard M. Ryan, 255–275. Rochester, NY: University of Rochester Press, 2002.

"Beane Happy to Run A's through 2008." *Sports Illustrated*, November 11, 2002

Berinato, Scott. "If You Want to Motivate Someone, Shut Up Already." *Harvard Business Review* 91, no. 7 (July/August 2013): 24–25.

Blanchard, Kenneth H. *Leading at a Higher Level: Blanchard on Leadership and Creating High Performing Organizations.* Upper Saddle River, NJ: FT Press, 2009.

Blanchard, K. and S. Fowler-Woodring. *Empowerment: Achieving Peak Performance through Self-Leadership.* Blanchard Family Partnership/Successories, Inc., 1998.

Blanchard, Kenneth H., Susan Fowler, and Laurence Hawkins. *Self Leadership and The One Minute Manager: Increasing Effectiveness through Situational Self Leadership.* New York: William Morrow, 2005.

Bronkhorst, Quinton. "Games vs. Movies: Who Wins?" BusinessTech, August 14, 2012. http://businesstech.com /news/general/19901/games-vs-movies-who-wins/.

Brown, Kirk W., and Melissa Holt. "Experiential Processing and the Integration of Bright and Dark Sides of the Human Psyche." In *Designing the Future of Positive Psychology: Taking Stock and Moving Forward*, edited by Kennon M. Sheldon, Todd B. Kashdan, and Michael F. Steger, 147–159. New York: Oxford University Press, 2011.

Brown, Kirk W., and Richard M. Ryan. "The Benefits of Being Present: Mindfulness and Its Role in Psychological Well-Being." *Journal of Personality and Social Psychology* 84, no. 4 (2003): 822–848.

Brown, Kirk W., Richard M. Ryan, and J. David Creswell. "Mindfulness: Theoretical Foundations and Evidence for Its Salutary Effects." *Psychological Inquiry* 18, no. 4 (2007): 211–237.

Burnette, J. L., E. M. VanEpps, E. J. Finkel, E. H. O'Boyle, and J. M. Pollack. "Mind-Sets Matter: A Meta-analytic Review of Implicit Theories and Self-Regulation." *Psychological Bulletin* 139, no. 3 (2013): 655–701.

Christakis, Nicholas A., and James H. Fowler. *Connected: The Surprising Power of Our Social Networks and How They Shape Our Lives—How Your Friends' Friends' Friends Affect Everything You Feel, Think, and Do*. New York: Back Bay Books, 2011.

Csikszentmihalyi, Mihaly. *Flow: The Psychology of Optimal Experience*. New York: Harper Perennial Modern Classics, 2008.

Deci, E. L., J. G. La Guardia, A. C. Moller, M. J. Scheiner, and R. M. Ryan. "On the Benefits of Giving as Well as Receiving Autonomy Support: Mutuality in Close Friendships." *Personality and Social Psychology Bulletin* 32, no. 3 (March 2006): 313–327.

Deci, Edward L., and Richard M. Ryan. "Facilitating Optimal Motivation and Psychological Well-Being across Life's Domains." *Canadian Psychology* 49, no. 1 (2008): 14–23.

————, eds. *Handbook of Self-Determination Research*. Rochester, NY: University of Rochester Press, 2002.

Deci, E. L., R. M. Ryan, M. Gagne, D. R. Leone, J. Usunov, and B. P. Kornazheva. "Need Satisfaction, Motivation, and Well-Being in the Work Organizations of a Former Eastern Bloc Country: A Cross-Cultural Study of Self-Determination." *Personality and Social Psychology Bulletin* 27, no. 8 (August 2001): 930–942.

Dweck, Carol. *Mindset: The New Psychology of Success.* New York: Ballantine Books, 2007.

Edmonds, Chris, and Lisa Zigarmi. *#Positivity at Work Tweet Book 01: 140 Bite-Sized Ideas to Help You Create a Positive Organization Where Employees Thrive.* Cupertino, CA: THINKaha, 2012.

Facer, D. C., Jr., F. Galloway, N. Inoue, and D. Zigarmi. "Creation and Initial Validation of the Motivation Beliefs Inventory: Measuring Leaders' Beliefs about Employee Motivation Using Four Motivation Theories." *Journal of Business Administration Research* 3, no. 1 (2014): 1–18. http://www.sciedu.ca/journal/index.php/jbar/article/view/3905.

Fehr, Ernst, and Suzann-Viola Renninger. "If We Live in a Dog-Eat-Dog World, Then Why Are We Frequently So Good to Each Other? The Samaritan Paradox." *Scientific American Mind* 14, no. 5 (2004): 15–21.

Frankl, Viktor E. *Man's Search for Meaning.* Boston: Beacon Press, 2006.

Gagne, M., E. Chemolli, J. Forest, and R. Koestner. "A Temporal Analysis of the Relation between Organizational Commitment and Work Motivation." *Psychologica Belgica* 48 no. 2–3 (2008): 219–241.

Gagne, Marylene, and Edward L. Deci. "Self-Determination Theory and Work Motivation." *Journal of Organizational Behavior* 26 (2005): 331–362.

Garfield, Charles. *Peak Performers: The New Heroes of American Business.* New York: William Morrow, 1987.

Gillet, Nicolas, Evelyne Fouquereau, Jacques Forset, Paul Brunault, and Philippe Columbat. "The Impact of Organizational Factors on Psychological Needs and Their

Relations with Well-Being." *Journal of Business Psychology* 27 (2012): 437–450.

Hagger, Martin S., Nikos L. D. Chatzisarantis, and Jemma Harris. "From Psychological Need Satisfaction to Intentional Behavior: Testing a Motivational Sequence in Two Behavioral Contexts." *Personality and Social Psychology Bulletin* 32, no. 2 (February 2006): 131–148.

Hitlin, Steven, and Jane A. Piliavin. "Values: Reviving a Dormant Concept." *Annual Review of Sociology* 30 (2004): 359–393.

Howe, Neil, and William Strauss. *Generations: The History of America's Future, 1584 to 2069.* Fort Mill, SC: Quill, 1992.

Irwin, Brandon C., Deborah L. Feltz, and Norbert L. Kerr. "Silence is Golden: Effect of Encouragement in Motivating the Weak Link in an Online Exercise Video Game." *Journal of Medical Internet Research* 15, no. 6 (2013): 1–10.

Jackson, Phil, and Hugh Delehanty. *Sacred Hoops: Spiritual Lessons of a Hardwood Warrior.* New York: Hyperion Books, 2006.

Jackson, Phil, and Hugh Delehanty. *Eleven Rings: The Soul of Success.* New York: Penguin Press, 2013.

Jenkins, Kim T., and Katy Tapper. "Resisting Chocolate Temptation Using a Brief Mindfulness Strategy." *British Journal of Health Psychology* (May 17, 2013): 1–14.

Kasser, Tim. *The High Price of Materialism.* Chester, NJ: Bradford Book Company, 2003.

Kennedy, Kelly. "Firms Bet Money Will Prod Employees to Health." *USA Today*, November 25, 2011.

Kerr, Norbert L., Deborah L. Feltz, and Brandon C. Irwin. "To Pay or Not to Pay? Do Extrinsic Incentives Alter the Kohler Group Motivation Gain?" *Group Processes and Intergroup Relations* (2012): 1–12.

Kidd, Celeste, Holly Palmeri, and Richard N. Aslin. "Rational Snacking: Young Children's Decision-Making on the Marshmallow Task Is Moderated by Beliefs about Environmental Reliability." *Cognition* 126, no. 1 (2013): 109–114.

Kleinginna, Paul R., Jr., and Anne M. Kleinginna. "A Categorized List of Motivation Definitions, with a Suggestion for a Consensual Definition." *Motivation and Emotion* 5, no. 3 (1981): 263–291.

Kohn, Alfie. *Punished by Rewards: The Trouble with Gold Stars, Incentive Plans, A's, Praise, and Other Bribes.* 2nd ed. Boston: Mariner Books, 1999.

Kotsou, I., J. Gregoire, M. Mikolajczak, and D. Nelis. "Emotional Plasticity: Conditions and Effects of Improving Emotional Competence in Adulthood." *American Psychological Association* 96, no. 4 (2011): 827–839.

Kovach, Kenneth. A. "Why Motivational Theories Don't Work." *Society for Advancement of Management* 45, no. 2 (Spring 1980): 54–59.

Meyer, John P., and Marylene Gagne. "Employee Engagement from a Self-Determination Theory Perspective." *Industrial and Organizational Psychology* 1, no. 1 (2008): 60–62.

Milyavskaya, Marina, I. Gingras, G. Mageau, R. Koestner, H. Gagnon, J. Fang, and J. Boiche. "Balance across Contexts: Importance of Balanced Need Satisfaction across Various Life Domains." *Personal Social Psychology Bulletin* 35, no. 8 (2009): 1031–1045.

Mischel, Walter, Ebbe B. Ebbesen, and Antonette R. Zeiss. "Cognitive and Attentional Mechanisms in Delay of Gratification." *Journal of Personality and Social Psychology* 21, no. 2 (1972): 204–218.

Mischel, Walter, Yuichi Shoda, and Monica L. Rodriguez. "Delay of Gratification in Children." *Science* 244, no. 4907 (May 26, 1989): 933–938.

Moller, A. C., H. G. McFadden, D. Hedeker, and B. Spring. "Financial Motivation Undermines Maintenance in an Intensive Diet and Activity Intervention." *Journal of Obesity* 2012 (2012): 1–8.

Murayama, K., M. Matsumoto, K. Izuma, and K. Matsumoto. "Neural Basis of the Undermining Effect of Monetary Reward on Intrinsic Motivation." *Proceedings of the National Academy*

of Sciences of the United States of America 107, no. 49
(October 2010): 1–6.

Nimon, Kim, and Drea Zigarmi. "The Work Cognition
Inventory—Revised." *Journal of Career Assessment*
(forthcoming).

Page, Kathryn M., and Dianne A. Vella-Brodrick. "The 'What,'
'Why' and 'How' of Employee Well-Being: A New Model."
Social Indicators Research 90 (2009): 441–458.

Patall, Erika A., Harris Cooper, and Jorgianne C. Robinson.
"The Effects of Choice on Intrinsic Motivation and Related
Outcomes: A Meta-analysis of Research Findings."
Psychological Bulletin 134, no. 2 (2008): 270–300.

Pink, Daniel H. *Drive: The Surprising Truth about What
Motivates Us.* New York: Riverhead Books, 2011.

Radel, R., P. Sarrazin, L. G. Pelletier, and M. Milyavskaya.
"Restoration Process of the Need for Autonomy: The Early
Alarm Stage." *Journal of Personality and Social Psychology*
101, no. 5 (2011): 919–934.

Reeve, Johnmarshall. *Understanding Motivation and Emotion.*
5th ed. Hoboken, NJ: Wiley, 2008.

Rigby, Scott, and Richard Ryan. *Glued to Games: How Video
Games Draw Us In and Hold Us Spellbound.* Santa Barbara:
Praeger, 2011.

Rock, David. *Your Brain at Work: Strategies for Overcoming
Distraction, Regaining Focus, and Working Smarter All Day
Long.* New York: Harper Business, 2009.

Ryan, Richard M., Jessey H. Bernstein, and Kirk W. Brown.
"Weekends, Work, and Well-Being: Psychological Need
Satisfactions and Day of the Week Effects on Mood, Vitality,
and Physical Symptoms." *Journal of Social and Clinical
Psychology* 29, no. 1 (2010): 95–122.

Ryan, Richard M., and James P. Connell. "Perceived Locus of
Causality and Internalization: Examining Reasons for Acting
in Two Domains." *Journal of Personality and Social
Psychology* 57, no. 5 (1989): 749–761.

Ryan, Richard M., and Edward L. Deci. "From Ego Depletion to Vitality: Theory and Findings Concerning the Facilitation of Energy Available to the Self." *Social and Personality Psychology Compass* 2, no. 2 (2008): 702–717.

―――――. "Self-Determination Theory and the Facilitation of Intrinsic Motivation, Social Development, and Well-Being." *American Psychologist* 55, no. 1 (January 2000): 68–78.

Ryback, David. "Self-Determination and the Neurology of Mindfulness." *Journal of Humanistic Psychology* 46, no. 4 (October 2006): 474–493.

Schlam, T. R., N. L. Wilson, Y. Shoda, W. Mischel, and O. Ayduk. "Preschoolers' Delay of Gratification Predicts Their Body Mass 30 Years Later." *Journal of Pediatrics* 162, no. 1 (2013): 90–93.

Sheldon, Kennon, Richard M. Ryan, Edward L. Deci, and Tim Kasser. "The Independent Effects of Goal Contents and Motives on Well-Being: It's Both What You Pursue and Why You Pursue It." *Personality and Social Psychology Bulletin* 30, no. 4 (April 2004): 475–486.

Smith, J. Walker, and Ann Clurman. *Generation Ageless*. New York: HarperCollins, 2007.

Tay, Louise, and Ed Diener. "Needs and Subjective Well-Being around the World." *Journal of Personality and Social Psychology* 101, no. 2 (2011): 354–365.

Vohs, Kathleen D., and Roy F. Baumeister. *Handbook of Self-Regulation: Research, Theory, and Applications.* 2nd ed. New York: Guilford Press, 2013.

Yamaguchi, Billy. *Billy Yamaguchi Feng Shui Beauty: Bringing the Ancient Principles of Balance and Harmony to Your Hair, Makeup and Personal Style.* Naperville: Sourcebooks, 2004.

Zigarmi, Drea, Kenneth H. Blanchard, Michael O'Connor, and Carl Edeburn. *The Leader Within: Learning Enough about Yourself to Lead Others Within.* Upper Saddle River, NJ: FT Press, 2004.

Zigarmi, Drea, Scott Blanchard, Vickie Essary, and Dobie
    Houson. *The Leadership-Profit Chain*. Escondido, CA:
    Ken Blanchard Companies, 2006.

Zigarmi, Drea, Susan Fowler, and Dick Lyles. *Achieve Leadership
    Genius*. Upper Saddle River, NJ: Financial Times Prentice
    Hall, 2008.

Zigarmi, Drea, and K. Nimon. "A Cognitive Approach to Work
    Intention: The Stuff That Employee Work Passion Is Made
    Of?" *Advances in Human Resources Development* 13, no. 4
    (2011): 443–457.

Zigarmi, Drea, K. Nimon, D. Houson, D. Witt, and J. Diehl.
    "Beyond Engagement: Toward a Framework and Operational
    Definition for Employee Passion." *Human Resource
    Development Review* 8, no. 3 (2009): 300–316.

————. "A Preliminary Field Test of an Employee Work Passion
    Model." *Human Resource Development Quarterly* 22, no. 2
    (2011): 195–221.

Zigarmi, Drea, and Taylor P. Roberts. "Leader Values as
    Predictors of Employee Affect and Work Passion Intentions."
    Journal of Modern Economy and Management 1, no. 1 (2012):
    1–32.

• Acknowledgments

Each of us is responsible for the quality of our own motivational outlook, but the people we associate with make a difference in the self-regulation required to experience optimal motivation.

Some of the people acknowledged here entered my life serendipitously, while others were consciously chosen. They all helped me create this wonderful life through their encouragement, insight, and support. My hope is that in some small way, the feeling is mutual. (My other hope is that if you are missing from this list, you will forgive me and trust that you are valued.)

My family at the Ken Blanchard Companies:

- These ideas would still be a dream if not for our Optimal Motivation product development team, Jay C., Vanessa G., Kelie S., Mike G., and most especially Gary Onstad and Victoria Cutler.

- My CHOMP (Community of Healthy Optimal Motivational Practitioners) colleagues, especially Els K., Judith D., Calla C., Mark P., Peter B., Lael G., David C., John L., John H., Nancy B., Ursula L., Belinda B., and Jacqueline R.

- Brave business developers who were early adapters, especially Laurie R., Kyleen C., Humberto M., Carolyn G.,

Chad G., Debbie C., Stacy S., Jackie G., Wei T., John S., Jim O., Neal S, and Brenda N.

- Our global partners especially Rares, Majiek, Alexandra, and Spiros

- All the project managers and supporters such as Brent B., Janey F., Cathy H., and Joni W.

- Blanchard's marketing team—David W., Brian A., Wendy W., and Lisa M. Special shout out to Patrick P.

- Values-based clients who appear throughout this book with additional thanks to Eline L., Tom P., Josine P., Martin B., Suzanne K., and Cheryl M.

I could fill another book with names. Wonderful life, indeed!

- *The Catholic Leadership Institute*—Learning Leaders, Matt M., Fr. Bill, and Dan C.

- *Berrett-Koehler Publishers*—The reason this books exists, Neal M.; my shepherd, Jeevan S.; and the man behind BK's values, Steve P., and the production and marketing teams, especially Dianne P., Sharon G., Beverly B., Courtney S., Kristen F., Katie S., Kat E., Mike C., and Charlotte A.

- *Master of Science in Executive Leadership program at the University of San Diego*—Our students, faculty, and amazing team for a robust learning lab over the past fifteen years, especially Christina D., Gina F., and Bridget B.

- *Respected colleagues and creative collaborators*—Eileen H., Dick T., Trudy P., Jett B., Martha L., Kenny T., Jesse

S., Paula D., Chris E., Carol S., Phil R., Carey N., Ricardo M., Kurt G., and the SDT community, especially Jacques F. and Marylene G.

- *My "kids," who are all represented literally, figuratively, and lovingly throughout this book*—Alexa T., Blair C., Grant C., Lisa Z., Ryan T., and Evey T.

- My PR team—Cave Henricks Communications and Shelton Interactive—Barbara H., Rusty S., and Jessica K. Thank you to Weaving Influence—Becky R. and Kylah F.

Most importantly, my codevelopers of Optimal Motivation, Dr. David Facer and Dr. Drea Zigarmi:

- David's expertise and capacity to explore the depths of the ideas were invaluable to me personally and proved essential to the Spectrum of Motivation model and conceptual validity of the framework presented in this book. David helped take these ideas to a higher level.

- My forever partner, Drea Zigarmi, whose love and wisdom took my *life* to a higher level.

• Index

• Resources

The Ken Blanchard Companies

The Ken Blanchard Companies® is a global leader in workplace learning, productivity, performance, and leadership effectiveness that is best known for its Situational Leadership® II program—the most widely taught leadership model in the world. Blanchard's offerings are embraced by Fortune 500 companies as well as midsize to small-size businesses, governments, and educational and nonprofit organizations.

Blanchard® workshops and experiences that support the ideas in this book, include

- Optimal Motivation®

- Leading with Optimal Motivation

- Situational Leadership® II

- Situational Self Leadership

- DISCovering Self and Others

- Giving and Receiving Optimal Feedback

- Goal Setting

To inquire about Susan Fowler or other leadership experts for workshops and consulting as well as keynote addresses, please contact the Ken Blanchard Companies Global Headquarters:

125 State Place
Escondido, CA 92029
www.kenblanchard.com
1.800.728.6000 from the United States
+ 1.760.489.5005 from anywhere

More from Susan Fowler
Visit Susan's website for a free assessment, additional re-
sources, and blog posts at http://www.susanfowler.com.
You can find her books online and in bookstores, including

*   *Self Leadership and the One Minute Manager,*
    with Ken Blanchard and Laurence Hawkins

*   *Achieve Leadership Genius,* with Drea Zigarmi
    and Dick Lyles

*   *Leading at a Higher Level,* with Ken Blanchard
    and colleagues

*   *Good Leaders, Good Shepherds,* with Dick Lyles,
    Tim Flanagan, and Drea Zigarmi

    Susan is also a guest blogger at LeaderChat.org.

**David Facer, PhD—Leadership Coach, Adjunct Professor
at the University of San Diego, and Coauthor of Optimal
Motivation and the Spectrum of Motivation**
David Facer works with corporate executives and entrepreneurs to create breakthrough performance for themselves,
their teams, and the wider organization. This often involves
developing unique insight and skills to address the human
complexity in their organizations. His popular Activate

Potential blog can be found at http://www.activatepotential
.com, and you can learn more on his LinkedIn page, www
.linkedin.com/in/davidfacerexecutivecoach.

Drea Zigarmi—Coauthor of Optimal Motivation and the Spectrum of Motivation

Drea Zigarmi is the head of research and a founding associate of the Ken Blanchard Companies. You can contact him through the Blanchard website at www.kenblanchard.com regarding his latest academic journal publications. His book *The Leader Within*[1] is essential reading for anyone serious about leading with Optimal Motivation. He is currently working on a book about justice in the workplace.

Recommended Leadership Programs Incorporating Optimal Motivation Principles

- Masters of Science in Executive Leadership, University of San Diego, http://www.sandiego.edu/business/programs/ms-executive-leadership

- Good Leaders, Good Shepherds and Tending the Talents, Catholic Leadership Institute, http://www.catholicleaders.org

• About the Author

Susan Fowler is on a quest to help leaders at all levels flourish as they succeed. Widely known as one of the foremost experts on motivation and personal empowerment, Susan gained her knowledge through extensive experience in business, advertising, sales, production, marketing, executive and lifestyle coaching, and leadership training in all fifty states and forty foreign countries with clients as diverse as Google, Harley-Davidson, Kawasaki, Pfizer, Merck, T.J. Maxx, Reitmans of Canada, National Basketball Association, AkzoNobel, and Apple.

Susan is the coauthor of the innovative Optimal Motivation experiences for The Ken Blanchard Companies as well as the creator and lead developer of Situational Self Leadership, the organization's best-of-class self-leadership and personal empowerment program. She was given the Lifetime Achievement Award for instructional design from the North American Simulations and Gaming Association.

Susan is the coauthor of three books with Ken Blanchard: *Self Leadership and the One Minute Manager, Leading at a Higher Level*, and *Empowerment*. She coauthored *Achieve Leadership Genius, The Team Leader's Idea-a-Day Guide*, and *Good Leaders, Good Shepherds*. She also authored the audio programs *Overcoming Procrastination* and *Mentoring*.

Susan lives with her husband, Drea Zigarmi, in San Diego, where she is a senior consulting partner for the Ken Blanchard Companies, a leadership consultant and coach; and a professor in the Master of Science in Executive Leadership program at the University of San Diego. Susan is a rotating board member for Angel Faces, a nonprofit organization serving adolescent girls with severe burn trauma and disfigurements.

Berrett–Koehler
Publishers

Connecting people and ideas
to create a world that works for all

Dear Reader,

Thank you for picking up this book and joining our worldwide community of Berrett-Koehler readers. We share ideas that bring positive change into people's lives, organizations, and society.

To welcome you, we'd like to offer you a free e-book. You can pick from among twelve of our bestselling books by entering the promotional code **BKP92E** here: http://www.bkconnection.com/welcome.

When you claim your free e-book, we'll also send you a copy of our e-newsletter, the *BK Communiqué*. Although you're free to unsubscribe, there are many benefits to sticking around. In every issue of our newsletter you'll find

- A free e-book
- Tips from famous authors
- Discounts on spotlight titles
- Hilarious insider publishing news
- A chance to win a prize for answering a riddle

Best of all, our readers tell us, "Your newsletter is the only one I actually read." So claim your gift today, and please stay in touch!

Sincerely,

Charlotte Ashlock
Steward of the BK Website

Questions? Comments? Contact me at bkcommunity@bkpub.com.